Using
Massive
Digital
Libraries

Using
Massive
Digital
Libraries

A LITA Guide

Andrew Weiss

An imprint of the American Library Association

CHICAGO   2014

Andrew Weiss is the digital services librarian at the Oviatt Library, California State University, Northridge. His professional areas of expertise include scholarly communication, digital repository development, and open access advocacy. His past research has focused on digital libraries, digitization, and open access publishing. He also has great interest in the culture, literature, and history of librarianship in Japan. He earned his master's degree in library science from the University of Hawaii at Manoa.

Ryan James lives in Honolulu and works for the University of Hawai'i at Manoa Libraries. He is pursuing a PhD in Communications and Information Science.

© 2014 by the American Library Association.

Printed in the United States of America

18 17 16 15 14   5 4 3 2 1

Extensive effort has gone into ensuring the reliability of the information in this book; however, the publisher makes no warranty, express or implied, with respect to the material contained herein.

ISBNs: 978-0-8389-1235-5 (paper); 978-0-8389-1973-6 (PDF); 978-0-8389-1974-3 (ePub); 978-0-8389-9624-9 (Kindle). For more information on digital formats, visit the ALA Store at alastore.ala.org and select eEditions.

Library of Congress Cataloging-in-Publication Data
Weiss, Andrew, 1971-
        Using massive digital libraries : a LITA guide / Andrew Weiss. — First edition.
           pages cm. — (LITA guides)
        Includes bibliographical references and index.
        ISBN 978-0-8389-1235-5 (alk. paper)
        1. Digital libraries. 2. Libraries—Special collections—Computer network resources. 3. Libraries—Electronic information sources. 4. Scholarly electronic publishing. 5. Scholarly web sites. 6. Digital libraries—Collection development. 7. Google Library Project—Case studies. I. Library and Information Technology Association (U.S.). II. Title.
        Z4080W43 2014
        025.042—dc23   2014009541

Book design in Berkeley and Avenir. Cover image © Zeed/Shutterstok, Inc.

♾ This paper meets the requirements of ANSI/NISO Z39.48-1992 (Permanence of Paper).

To Akiko and Mia

Contents

▧ PART 3 ▧
Practical Applications

Preface

This book is a study of provocation and reactionism, futurism and its shifting paradigms, foretellings and forebodings, and above all else an examination of new worlds. In the past ten to fifteen years modern societies have undergone major shifts in how they accumulate, produce, and distribute information. Increasingly, the Internet is the primary source of our information, entertainment, news, gossip, and social interaction. What one might call "legacy" media (e.g., print newspapers, television, radio, telephony, and even aging digital formats like Zip drives, MO discs, DVDs, and the like) have endured some of the more visible challenges to their methods of creating and distributing information, and to the business models of the companies that distribute them. Other institutions have been equally affected, but in ways that are less visible or tangential to their core missions.

This book is an attempt to explore what libraries—one of the many institutions affected by these changes—will look like as the twenty-first century progresses. It is impossible to address all the pertinent issues in one volume, and no scholar of librarianship would claim to fully understand all the changes happening. Yet the pillars that support the library as one of civilization's "big ideas" are weaker now than they have ever been, having been eroded from external and internal forces that are economic, ideological, and legal in nature.

It is left to us to look to the far boundaries of current traditional library models and choose a newly developing area of library and information science that shows the promise of change, for good and for ill, in the field. It is hoped that the

---

Ryan James contributed to this preface.

exploration of one such narrow area will help provide insight into the possible wider changes that are likely to come in future decades.

This book examines what Ryan James and I in previous studies have together defined as massive digital libraries (MDLs). This term is still unsettled, having been coined only recently. However, the need for new terminology hinges upon the desire to describe what we believe to be a new class of digital libraries, which, though we admit are rooted in past models, are flourishing and will only grow larger and more influential.

A massive digital library is a collection of organized information large enough to rival the size of the world's largest bricks-and-mortar libraries in terms of book collections. The examples examined in this book range from hundreds of thousands of books to tens of millions. This basic definition of an MDL, however, is in some ways insufficient. It describes what an MDL is in some ways but says nothing about how it is similar and dissimilar from more traditional libraries. What we can use it for, then, is as a starting point for discussion. As the book progresses this definition is refined further to make it more usable and relevant. This book will introduce more characteristics of MDLs and examine how they affect the current traditional library.

The creation of MDLs has led to what might be called an existential crisis in librarianship. Some might say that MDLs will eventually lead to the end of traditional libraries. While this author agrees with this in part, I do not necessarily share the doom and gloom of some commenters.

There are very few traditional bricks-and-mortar libraries that can be lumped together into a single group with just one set of uniform characteristics identifying what the library should be. The library is instead a concept—the "big idea"—that has been implemented in many different ways for thousands of years. The newness of MDLs gives us a chance to critically examine these new entities to see how they fit within traditional librarianship while also allowing us to reexamine what a library is now and how it might change in the future.

MDLs are here to stay. They are part of the future. They are provocative on multiple fronts, challenging hidebound assumptions about the library's centrality as a space for study and the housing of physical books and volumes. If the concept of the library and its intellectual underpinnings are to persist in the foreseeable future, they will need to be adapted to the reality of current conditions to avoid diminishment. For those who believe such changes spell doom to the library as we know it, we can only suggest—with but the tiniest tip of the tongue in our cheek—that the proverbial canary may just as easily become the canard in the coal mine.

Some readers may disagree with the ideas and frameworks presented in this book. That is a good thing. We would prefer to provoke a spirited discussion of the topic in the hopes that MDLs gain both greater respect for their positive aspects and astute criticism for their missteps and overreaches.

We hope that readers will find that the need for the term *MDL* is here, as well as become more aware of the strengths and weaknesses of MDLs as digital information tools. Once librarians are able to understand what they are, how they function, and how they are created and aggregated, they can better assess them for multiple purposes. It is hoped also that those reading the book are perhaps inspired to develop new ways of researching MDLs. We hope a new generation of librarians will foster a new approach to these tools and consider developing their own.

We neither despair about the future nor approach it with naive enchantment. Our approach is based in curiosity. We wish to examine where we are, how we got here, and where we might be going. The goal is to explore the history of MDLs, what they currently are, and issues their creation raises for library science today. As for the future of libraries as a whole, we leave the writing of speculative fiction to others more imaginative than ourselves.

I would like to acknowledge the following people who made sections of this book possible: Akiko Gonoue Weiss, for her assistance with some Japanese translation; Elizabeth Altman and Eric Willis, for their help with the Google Books display web widget of the integrated library system (ILS) of California State University, Northridge; the staff and librarians at the Keio University–Mita Campus Libraries, for their hospitality and cooperation during the interview process; and Annaliese Taylor, Edward Fox, Paul Marchionini, and Paul Heald, for allowing the use and adaptation of their images.

SPECIAL ACKNOWLEDGMENT: DEVELOPING THE CONCEPT OF THE MASSIVE DIGITAL LIBRARY

I would like to acknowledge my debt to Ryan James, who has cowritten several chapters as well as this preface. Ryan has been central to the development and shaping of the book as well as its central concept. The idea of the massive digital library as outlined in this book is the result of numerous discussions between us over the course of several years. This book could not have been written without his valuable input, insight, and above all, friendship.

PART 1

Background

Chapter One

A Brief History of Libraries—
or, How Did We Get Here?

*And further, by these, my son, be admonished: of making many books
there is no end; and much study is a weariness of the flesh.*

—Ecclesiastes 12:12

ON THE BINDING PROPERTIES OF LIBRARIES—
KEEPING THE FORCES OF ENTROPY
AND DISORDER AT BAY

The ancient Greeks had an "app for that," or at least a story. From Pandora to
Prometheus the heroes in their myths have trouble with powerful inventions—by
misusing them, stealing them from peevish gods, or failing to grasp their future
ramifications. Theseus, for example, trapped in the Minotaur's maze, escaped only
by following a length string that Ariadne had secretly given him. That slender string
kept Theseus linked to the outside world as he penetrated deeper into Daedalus's
labyrinth and into the Minotaur's lair. Even though Theseus was eventually forced
to abandon Ariadne on the island of Naxos and inadvertently drove his father to
suicide, he was the lucky one. Everyone else who took on the maze and the Minotaur died in the process. We all know what happened to Daedalus's son, too, when
the father-son duo fled the half-crazed kingdom of Minos on wings made of wax
and feathers (Nowadays some precocious programmer might call this "i-carus,"
the app that guarantees digital filial obedience.)

In some ways the myth of Theseus mirrors the contemporary Internet user experience. The myth suggests that any system—be it physical, psychological, or informational—that confounds its users becomes a dangerous one. Losing the connection with the real world in the twists and turns of life is an experience akin to death. What is at stake in the current incarnation of the web is the basis of knowledgeable existence itself. When one can no longer draw the thread between pieces of verifiable information, meaning gets lost, and that loss of meaning contributes to the death of knowledge and the ultimate decline of a culture. Think "digital Dark Ages," but not as a loss of access to information—as an undifferentiated glut of bits and bytes jumbled together and reconstituted at will by unseen and unknown forces whose motives are not discernible.

Libraries have made the attempt for centuries to ensure that the strings binding information together remain intact. In the past, this was easier, as the amount of published and archival work was much lower and therefore more manageable. Binding books; creating physical spaces as safe repositories; and hand copying or printing multiple, high-quality versions were all effective ways of preserving knowledge and ensuring that it remained bound to its culture and rooted in truth.

Of course, the calamities of history—including the burning and ransacking of libraries; cultural revolutions; and even moths, roaches, and book beetles—have taken their toll on the strings binding traditions together. The lost works of Aristotle and the meager fragments of Sappho are but two examples of the Fate-severed strings of Western culture. The ancient library of Alexandria, which in its prime supposedly held five hundred thousand volumes within its walls, stands as the great example of a lost culture (Knuth 2003).

Yet even in antiquity people despaired at information overload and the lack of facile resource management. In her 2011 book *Too Much to Know: Managing Scholarly Information Before the Modern Age* Blair suggests that *every* age has had to deal with information overload.[1] Ecclesiastes 12:12 tells readers to be cautious of too many books.[2] Hippocrates in 400 BC tells us, "Ars longa, vita brevis, occasio praeceps, experimentum periculosum, iudicium difficile," which can be translated as "Technique long, life short, opportunity fleeting, experience perilous, and decision difficult." Contrary to the oversimplified translation "Art lasts, life [is] short," Hippocrates instead may have been suggesting that because the acquisition of a skill or a body of knowledge takes a long time, human life is too short in comparison, and the mind is too limited to wield all this learning to perfection.

By the thirteenth century learned people were trying to cope with ever more information. The Dominican Vincent of Beauvais laments on "the multitude of books, the shortness of time and the slipperiness of memory." The printing press was still two hundred years away, yet people felt dismay at the growth of information. The problem has only grown exponentially since then, even as new technologies have been developed to better meet the problems of information overload.

ENTER THE DIGITAL DRAGON

Jumping ahead to contemporary times, we see that digital technology, no less world altering than Gutenberg's printing press, has transformed information culture even more. Libraries have in turn made the necessary transition from the physical world to the virtual world, but this technological shift brings practical and philosophical changes. Where the past model for libraries was based on scarcity, new models are based on abundance. Dempsey describes current libraries as moving from an "outside-in" model, in which resources are collected in situ, to an "inside-out" model, in which access points may be available within a library but the actual resources exist outside its walls.[3]

In the past, libraries struggled to provide as many informational sources as they could with the resources they had. Now, with online resources—some open, but most proprietary in nature—dominating the information landscape, libraries have had to cope with the proverbial water hose turned on at full blast. On the one hand, the amount of information available has increased beyond anyone's imagination. Services such as Wikipedia, Google Books, and Internet Archive, as well as the open access movement, with its gold open access journals and green open access repositories have each removed many of the barriers to information, especially location and cost. On the other hand, access to information without the ability to distinguish quality, relevancy, and overall comprehensiveness diminishes its impact.

THE DIGITAL LIBRARY—EARLY VISIONS

The discussion thus far has been limited primarily to resource access and the problems of information management in traditional bricks-and-mortar libraries, with a brief nod toward digital models. However, this doesn't address where the idea for a virtual library began. Certain technologies, economies of scale, and societal advancements needed to exist before the dream of a digital library (DL) could be

5

realized. As in all historical events that seem inevitable, we will see that a large number of developments had to occur simultaneously before the final product could be realized.

The digital library wouldn't exist without the modern fundamental concept and philosophy of the term *digital*. While this is a word that appears even in Middle English—referring mostly to counting numbers less than ten fingers—according to the online version of *Oxford English Dictionary* (www.oed.com), the first mention of the modern concept of digital is in the US Patent 2,207,537 from 1940, which defined the idea as "the transmission of direct current digital impulses over a long line the characteristics of the line tend to mutilate the wave shape." From this patent, essentially redefining the word as a series of on-off, zero-one switches, the modern digital era was born.

The idea for the first digital library, however, is a little more difficult to pin down. The first mention, and likely most influential inspiration for modern computing, is the Memex from Vannevar Bush's well-known 1945 article "As We May Think." Bush described his invention:

> [It is] a device in which an individual stores all his books, records, and communications, and which is mechanized so that it may be consulted with exceeding speed and flexibility. It is an enlarged intimate supplement to his memory.
>
> It consists of a desk, and while it can presumably be operated from a distance, it is primarily the piece of furniture at which he works. On the top are slanting translucent screens, on which material can be projected for convenient reading. There is a keyboard, and sets of buttons and levers. Otherwise it looks like an ordinary desk.[4]

He provides an astonishingly clear approximation of what the desktop personal computer eventually became in the 1980s and 1990s. However, this vision and its reality took some time to meet in the middle.

By the 1950s and 1960s visions of an electronic or digital library—much clearer than Vannevar Bush's vision—start to come into focus. Looking at Licklider's *Libraries of the Future* from 1965, one can start to see the engineer-centric philosophy of stripping away the book and print materials as an information delivery system from the core of library services. Licklider shows an apt prescience for the main issues of contemporary information science:

> We delimited the scope of the study, almost at the outset, to functions, classes of information, and domains of knowledge in which *the items of basic interest are not the print or paper, and not the words and sentences themselves—but the facts, concepts, principles, and ideas that lie behind the visible and tangible aspects of documents.* (Licklider 1965, my emphasis)

Working in an era of limited computing capacity as well as minimal digital imaging, Licklider and his colleagues were concerned with the transmission of the essential components of the document, be it literature, scholarship, or even a basic list. In other words, they focused on the book's data and metadata, its context, and its information, establishing the way that most digital projects would later handle texts, by stripping them of the extraneous physical properties that interfere with the so-called purity of the information conveyed. It also points toward document descriptions and other text markup strategies, such as XML, HTML, and XHTML, that later become standards in the field.

Licklider is especially prescient in his suggestion that libraries of the future should not focus as much on physical methods of information delivery—on the "freight and storage" as Douglas Englebart called it in 1963—such as the book and the physical bookshelf, which are, in his mind, incredibly inefficient on a mass scale. Instead, libraries should reject these physical trappings in favor of better methods of information and information processing. The future was promising for what he called "precognitive systems," which later became the basis of information retrieval (Licklider 1965; Sapp 2002).

He also writes, somewhat reminiscent of Bush in 1945, that engineers "need to substitute for the book a device that will make it easy to transmit information without transporting material, and that will not only present information to people but also process it for them" (Licklider 1965, 6). Here he anticipates what eventually became machine-readable text schemas, but it took at least a generation, beginning in the 1960s with the invention of ASCII code, and running through the 1970s and 1980s, to fully incorporate the digital into this new "text cycle." Project Gutenberg, one of the original digital libraries to focus on print books, is a great example of the types of digital library stemming from this period.[5]

The 1970s and 1980s were essential in the development of the tools that would help with the generation of digital texts. As Hillesund and Noring (2006, para. 9) write, "By the 1970s, keyboards and computer screens became the interface between man and computer. Beginning in the 1980s, powerful word processors and desktop publishing applications were developed. The writing and production phases of the text cycle were thus digitized, but the applications were primarily designed to facilitate print production."

Information retrieval systems began at this time as well with the appearance of Lexis for legal information, Dialog, Orbit, and BRS/Search systems (Lesk 2012). Even though the Library of Congress had pioneered electronic book indexing with the MARC record in 1969, it wasn't until the 1980s that the online catalog became widespread (Lesk 2012). By the early 1990s the field of information retrieval and its dream of the digital library were on their way to full realization.

DIGITAL LIBRARIES—THE VISION BECOMES A (VIRTUAL) REALITY

When Edward Fox in 1993 looked back on his early days at Massachusetts Institute of Technology (MIT) under Licklider, he was able to say with great certainty that "technological advances in computing and communication now make digital libraries feasible; economic and political motivation make them inevitable" (79). He had good reason to be optimistic in his assessment. By this point in time ARPAnet had been around for twenty-four years, the Internet had been born, hypertext developed as a force in the 1980s under such projects as Ted Nelson's Xanadu, Brown University's IRIS Project, and Apple's HyperCard (Fox 1993). The 1990s also saw the development of the HTML protocol, which then gave way to XML and its strong, yet interoperable, framework (Fox 1993). Along with the philosophical framework and software development in the 1980s and 1990s, there was also developing a solid information infrastructure and network from such schemes as Ethernet, asynchronous transfer modes that pushed data transfer speeds from thousands of bits per second to billions (Fox 1993).

By the early to mid-1990s many publishers, libraries, and universities were able to try their hand at creating their own digital collections. Oxford began the Oxford Text Archive, the Library of Congress developed its American Memory Project, and even the French government had planned to digitally scan one million books in the French National Library (Fox 1993).

At this time, multiple visions of what a digital library might entail were also beginning to take form. A digital library was at this point "a broad term encompassing scholarly archives, text collections, cultural heritage, and educational resource sites" (Hillesund and Noring 2006, para. 1). There was little consensus on a specific application and definition. Yet many of the common signposts on the current library digital landscape were in their infancy by this time, and each provided a distinct and important model for a DL. For example, a proto–subject repository for computer science departments to share, archive, and provide search functions for technical reports was developed as a joint project between Virginia Tech, Old Dominion, and SUNY Buffalo. The University of Michigan was pioneering electronic theses and dissertations, and Carnegie Mellon, a full eleven years before Google's book digitization announcement, was already looking into "distributed digital libraries" with its Plexus Project, with the goal of "developing large-scale digital libraries using hypermedia technology" (Akscyn and McCracken 1993, 11).

DIGITAL LIBRARIES—UNEVEN GROWTH, WEB 2.0, AND EXPANDING DEFINITIONS

By the late 1990s, however, the landscape had grown by leaps and bounds. Google had entered the fray with its revolutionary search engine algorithm, the Internet had exploded on the scene and into most homes, MIT had developed its first DSpace institutional repository system, and e-books were in their infancy.

In examining the landscape of the digital library (which most practitioners now called "DL") as it was in 1999, Marchionini and Fox (1999) noted that digital libraries had entered a second phase, though they had also begun to see some lags in the development of digital libraries. They posited four specific dimensions in the progress of digital libraries: community, technology, services, and content.

As figure 1.1 demonstrates, in their estimation, "progress along these [four] dimensions is uneven, mainly driven by work in technology and content with research and development related to services and especially community lagging" (Marchionini and Fox 1999, 219).

It has turned out that a viable "community," the element most lagging in this depiction, was really just around the corner. Web 2.0, or social media, was the missing ingredient in the development of digital libraries and their applicability to particular communities. Digital projects would wind up better serving communities by utilizing such technologies as RSS feeds, Twitter, Facebook, and the other multiple "social" web applications.

The definition of the digital library had expanded by the early 2000s to include a large number of online initiatives and digitization projects that included things such

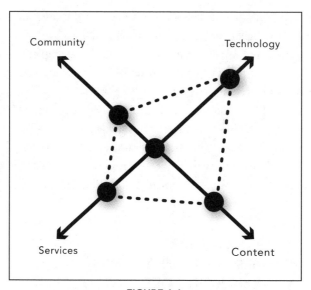

FIGURE 1.1
The four dimensions of digital library progress.
Image redrawn with permission by authors after Marchionini and Fox (1999).

as archival collections, cultural sites, educational resources, and even institutional repositories.

Scholarly archives included digital collections of scanned materials, such as a digital archive, collections of published and unpublished materials, as well as finding aids and other digital text initiatives. Open educational resource sites such as MERLOT and the California Digital Library began to gather learning objects, university scholarship, and other class-related materials. Institutional repositories, which had begun in the late 1990s, burgeoned once an open-source software solution, DSpace, became widely available and supported by various initiatives. Many institutional repository's collections contain university theses and dissertations (both digitized and born digital), as well as digitized books and book chapters, in addition to the usual peer-reviewed faculty journal articles. These disparate collections of material constitute digital libraries in the sense that they are gathering digital images and OCR text together and indexing them for complex searching (Lesk 2012).

A typical example of the digital library emerging during this phase of development was the International Children's Digital Library (http://en.childrenslibrary.org). This project initially began with about 1,000 digitized children's books. It expanded from that time to more than 4,600 books. Its organization has taken care to curate a small but diverse collection of children's books. It also devised uniquely child-centric methods of searching, including employing a bright, cartoonish user interface and developing a search to identify books by the color of their covers

DIGITAL LIBRARIES—E-BOOKS, MDLS, AND DUSTBINS

Once social media began to affect online accessibility and change how users approached online content, digital libraries reached a critical mass. Around 2005 the aggregation of content from various sources—crowdsourcing, in a sense— began to have an impact on content development. This, as we will see in the next chapter, was spurred in large part by Google and its ambitious announcement that it would digitize every book in the world (Jeanneney 2007).

However, along with the current aggregation of digitized content, born-digital books have also begun to drive content development. At the present date, e-books and their content-delivery hardware devices are starting to finally take off as viable alternatives to print books. In one study released in 2012, the number of Americans using e-books increased from 16 percent to 23 percent in one year.[6] It may be that the third phase of the digital library will also see the simultaneous development of mobile devices providing access to the traditional bound long-form narrative. Already books of many types—including directories, textbooks, trade publications, and travel guides—are born digital. This lack of physical form will have a profound impact on the way that people use and process "linear, narrative book-length treatments" (Hahn 2008, 20). Certainly new technologies are adopted and adapted in ways that their original creators never intended. It remains to be seen how and in what manner these technologies will be implemented most effectively.

To end this section, it is important to remember that cautionary tales exist even in the digital library world, despite its relatively recent appearance. One of the largest digitization projects during the late 1990s and early 2000s was Carnegie Mellon's Million Books Project. By 2007, it had finished its mission of digitizing and placing online a full collection of books in various languages. Unfortunately, much like the ICDL and its small-scale collection, the Million Books Project has been superseded by the next generation of massive digital libraries. Currently the software and servers for the Million Books Project—now known as the Universal Digital Library (www.ulib.org)—are not well maintained. Sustainability, so eloquently defined and described on the Universal Digital Library's

11

informational pages, is proving to be much less possible than anticipated. The unclear fate of this project—it's still available online but has neither been updated nor improved upon—provides us a glimpse into the likely future of many current digital projects. They become more examples of technology relegated to Trotsky's "dustbin of history," now providing more of a precariously unstable web history lesson than a useful service.

REFERENCES

Akscyn, Robert, and Donald McCracken. "PLEXUS: A Hypermedia Architecture for Large-Scale Digital Libraries." In *SIGDOC '93: Proceedings of the 11th Annual International Conference on Systems Documentation*, 11–20. New York: Association for Computing Machinery, 1993. doi: 10.1145/166025.166028.

Englebart, Douglas. 1963. "A Conceptual Framework for the Augmentation of Man's Intellect." In *Vistas in Information Handling*, edited by P. Howerton and D. Weeks, 1:1–29. Washington, DC: Spartan Books.

Fox, Edward. 1993. "Digital Libraries." *IEEE Computer* 26, no. 11: 79–81.

Hahn, Trudi Bellardo. 2008. "Mass Digitization: Implications for Preserving the Scholarly Record." *Library Resources and Technical Services* 52, no. 1: 18–26.

Hillesund, Terje, and Jon E. Noring. 2006. "Digital Libraries and the Need for a Universal Digital Publication Format." *Journal of Electronic Publishing* 9, no. 2.

Jeanneney, Jean-Noël. 2007. *Google and the Myth of Universal Knowledge: A View from Europe*. Chicago: University of Chicago Press. First published in French in 2005.

Knuth, Rebecca. 2003. *Libricide: The Regime-Sponsored Destruction of Books and Libraries in the Twentieth Century*. Westport, CT: Praeger.

Lesk, Michael. 2012. "A Personal History of Digital Libraries." *Library Hi Tech 30*, no. 4: 592–603.

Licklider, J. C. R. 1965. *Libraries of the Future*. Cambridge, MA: MIT Press.

Marchionini, Gary, and Edward A. Fox. 1999. "Progress toward Digital Libraries: Augmentation through Integration." *Information Processing and Management* 35, no. 3: 219–225.

Sapp, Gregg. 2002. *A Brief History of the Future of Libraries: An Annotated Bibliography*. Lanham, MD: Scarecrow Press.

NOTES

1. See Jacob Soll, "Note This," review of *Too Much to Know: Managing Scholarly Information before the Modern Age*, by Ann M. Blair, *New Republic*, August 24, 2011, www.newrepublic.com/article/books-and-arts/magazine/94175/ann-blair-managing -scholarly-information.

2. Ann Blair, "Information Overload's 2,300-Year-Old History," *HBR Blog Network* (blog), http://blogs.hbr.org/cs/2011/03/information_overloads_2300-yea.html.

3. Lorcan Dempsey, "'The Inside Out Library: Scale, Learning, Engagement': Slides Explain How Today's Libraries Can More Effectively Respond to Change," *OCLC Research*, February 5, 2013, www.oclc.org/research/news/2013/02-05.html.

4. Vannevar Bush, "As We May Think," *Atlantic Monthly*, July 1945, www.theatlantic.com/magazine/archive/1945/07/as-we-may-think/303881/.

5. Michael Hart, "The History and Philosophy of Project Gutenberg," *Project Gutenberg*, August 1992, www.gutenberg.org/wiki/Gutenberg:The_History_and_Philosophy _of_Project_Gutenberg_by_Michael_Hart.

6. Lee Rainie and Maeve Duggan, "E-Book Reading Jumps; Print Book Reading Declines," Pew Internet and American Life Project, December 27, 2012, http://libraries.pewinternet.org/2012/12/27/e-book-reading-jumps-print-book-reading -declines/.

Chapter Two

Massive Digital Libraries— or, Where Are We?

Me, poor man, my library / Was dukedom large enough.

—William Shakespeare, *The Tempest*

DEFINING THE MASSIVE DIGITAL LIBRARY

This chapter examines the intellectual and theoretical assumptions about digital libraries to explain the need for establishing the massive digital library (MDL) as a differentiating concept. In previous publications, authors introduced this term to describe the digital libraries they analyzed in their work, including Google Books, HathiTrust, Internet Archive, and the Open Content Alliance (Weiss and James 2013a, 2013b). This term has proved to be useful in distinguishing the subjects from digital libraries in general, but further elucidation is warranted.

This brings us to the question, how does one define a massive digital library? To answer this question in depth, we must first look at the development of the digital library from the twenty-first century onward through multiple perspectives: collection sizes, methods of acquisition and collection development, collection content, collection diversity, content accessibility, metadata, and means of digital preservation.

There are fundamental questions to be explored, as well, such as the following: What is a library? How is an MDL different from the libraries of the twentieth century? Libraries are created to serve particular communities often limited by

Ryan James contributed to this chapter.

geography or intellectual discipline, but MDLs offer the promise of transcending these boundaries. Does size mater? If an MDL has some twenty million books but lacks the specific book a reader wants, of what worth is it? More broadly, if an MDL does not have significant coverage of a topic or subject, is it really better than a collection that focuses more narrowly?

These questions are not easy to answer.

FOUNDATIONS OF THE MDL

A Resounding Announcement

In late 2004 Google made its well-documented "resounding announcement," as Jean-Noël Jeanneney described it in his 2005 book *Google and the Myth of Universal Knowledge* (published originally in French, and then in 2007 translated to English), to digitize millions of the world's books—including works still in copyright—and to place them online. Jeanneney and others took the Google announcement as a wake-up call for European countries to catch up to the US company, whose motives were seen as not entirely trustworthy.

Nearly ten years on, however, it is hard to imagine as we ride the full wave of Web 2.0 dominated by Google and Facebook that their desire to create an online digital library should have come as such a shock. It is not as if Google altered or reinterpreted the fundamental concepts of the digital library or electronic document delivery. In looking at the development of the digital library, most of its ambitions, as well as the procedures to do so, had been either explicitly stated or hinted at in the various "library of the future" ventures that had begun as early as the 1950s and 1960s (Licklider 1965). Yet the shock and awe of Google's announcement caused significant hand-wringing and soul-searching at the time (Jeanneney 2007; Venkatraman 2009).

It is more likely that Jeanneney and others reacted to being caught flat footed and falling behind in terms of organization and ambition. The pushback was partly one of conservatism—not in the US political sense of the word, but in the urge to preserve current cultural values—and a distrust of the ways in which US-centric capitalism creates huge shifts in society and leaves many, especially those in other countries, in the lurch. There was also a quite justifiable realization that the social construct of the library itself, and the social contract upon which it has been built, could be endangered by such destabilizing projects.

Indeed, Google's main stated goal for the project, "to create a comprehensive, searchable, virtual card catalog," hints at deep shifts in the impact of the digital economy and capitalism itself.[1] An interview with Jaron Lanier, the computer scientist who coined the term *virtual reality*, drives home how revolutionary the Google Books initiative might really be for capitalist-driven societies:

> At the turn of the [twenty-first] century it was really Sergey Brin at Google who just had the thought . . . if we give away all the information services, but we make money from advertising, we can make information free and still have capitalism. But the problem with that is it reneges on the social contract where people still participate in the formal economy.[2]

As the formal economy—a regulated and documented exchange of goods, services, and labor—gravitates toward the informal economy of social media, where a clear exchange of money for goods and services created is not visible and users often provide the unpaid labor, the gestation and formation of new digital initiatives has the potential to be highly disruptive.

It is hard not to see the current rush to create similar digital library projects in this light. Although it is outside this book's overall scope to deeply examine these shifts, the informal economy's foray into digital libraries will surely influence whether bricks-and-mortar libraries remain relevant in the future information society. If people freely provide labor or tasks similar to what librarians traditionally have done, *even if they are ultimately inferior in quality*, then librarians will eventually become obsolete.

By the time Google made its proclamation to enter the digital library world, ambitiously taking on the task of digitizing millions of books, it was clear that digital library projects would be entering a new, third phase.[3] In Hahn's (2008) eyes, it is because companies that had never before stated an interest in joining the scholarly publication community (namely Google, Yahoo, and Microsoft) suddenly entered the fray that this major hand-wringing from the traditional stakeholders in scholarly communication resulted (i.e., libraries, publishers, scholars, cultural ministries, and governments). Where the previous interest of such companies was mainly in platforms, networks, hardware, and software applications, they now began to shift toward the "informalization" of previously unavailable and restricted content. Ironically, without the major involvement of companies and the gathering of various stakeholders the future of the digital library is very much unclear. Yet it is also compromised with them involved. The confluences of culture, technology,

17

community, services, and content itself are gathering together and barreling forth into the future, but their outcomes are very much unresolved.

The issues of information integrity and accessibility raised by the increasing economies of scale evinced in these new businesses entering the digital library game were addressed in part by the "very large digital library" (VLDL) movement, a precursor to the MDL in terms of nomenclature and classification. This movement took up the task of attempting to define and delineate some of the projects described here. From 2007 to 2011 workshops on VLDLs took place, attempting "to provide researchers, vendors, practitioners, application developers and users operating in the field of VLDLs with a forum fostering a constructive confront on the issues they face and the solutions they develop."[4] This theoretical approach includes examining "foundational, organization and systemic challenges" of digital libraries and their issues related to scalability, interoperability and sustainability.[5] However, the movement does not seem to have progressed beyond the most recent workshop, which was held in September 2011 in conjunction with the International Conference on Theory and Practice of Digital Libraries.

In some ways, the VLDL concept anticipates the definition in this book of the MDL, yet the term does not seem to have caught on, nor does the movement appear to be having much impact. Some of the problem may be that advocates for the movement admit to not having a "consensus yet on what a VLDL is" beyond a description of digital libraries that hold more than a specific amount of digital information.[6] Additionally, they appear to be approaching the problem purely from a computer science and computer engineering perspective, which may be limiting the appeal of the movement.

Giuseppe Amato's discussion of the social media digital-image site Flickr in the presentation "Dealing with Very Large Visual Document Archives" is an example of this.[7] While the work is of high caliber and provides excellent suggestions for utilizing shape recognition for searching images, it does make some missteps in terms of defining Flickr as an archive. It is not. To conflate the very specific LIS definition of an archive with that of an online social media image and content management system is to ignore many of the important tenets of librarianship. This makes the adoption of a term much more unlikely by a wider audience when boundaries and distinctions are not as clear as they could be.

Importantly, the VLDL movement does look at concepts such as volume and velocity, and variety of collections, yet its advocates admit that "there is not yet any threshold or indicator with respect to these features . . . that might be used to clearly discriminate very large digital libraries from digital libraries."[8] Therefore, incorporating some of the traditional aspects of librarianship, including both the digital and the bricks-and-mortar variations, will not only expand the interest in such MDL systems but also help to include predefined conceptions of archives, libraries, and asset management systems. These characteristics will help to define a new class of digital library.

Looking at Past Models as a Framework for MDLs

In many ways MDLs are the logical progression of the first digital libraries. In 1995 Fox and colleagues made the point that the digital library was defined differently by different constituents. The MDL may be no different. First, many have seen it as a result of new library functions, and Akscyn and colleagues (1995) note well the hyperbole that occurs when new technologies appear. New technologies tend to lead people to decide that the previous technologies are doomed to be replaced completely. But this has not been the case with television, radio, CDs, LPs, and other mature technologies. The same will be the case with digital libraries even as the massive digital libraries begin to aggregate more content and replace some of the value that users have come to see in them (Ishizuka 2005).

There is, of course, the danger that massive digital libraries will develop into something that does not serve the user in the same ways that more traditional libraries have. New technologies often bring forth conflicting feelings of excitement and trepidation among users. Professional librarians experience this acutely when they see the potential benefits that MDLs and other digital libraries promise, yet there is an underlying perceived threat to their profession.

In the early days, people viewed digital libraries as merely computerized versions of the physical library. Automation would fulfill this criterion quite easily. People also saw the digital library as offering new information resources. These new types of resources turned out to be a combination of various file formats, including video, audio, and web pages. Along with these definitions, we are also confronted with the digital library as the basis for new approaches to classification and cataloging. The Dublin Core Element Set, with its series of extensions and elaborations—Goddard Core and Darwin Core, for example—fits within this new type of library.

The digital library also suggests that there will be new modes of interaction with patrons. Instead of purely a face-to-face interaction or a physical locality defining the user (i.e., a community of users defined by proximity to a physical building), users and target audiences are spread out and further diffused. The result is a wider profile of users, which will ultimately affect collection development decisions and policies.

Mass digitization projects have been around for some time. The digital initiatives at the Library of Congress American Memory project, for example, and numerous long-term archival digitization projects provided the blueprints for large digital creation from the 1990s.[9] Institutional repositories have begun to create larger collections. According to current statistics from the Registry of Open Access Repositories (http://roar.eprints.org), the largest institutional repositories, or IRs (e.g., Networked Digital Library of Theses and Dissertations Union Catalog and Virtual Library of Historical Press) each contain more than a million items. However, as Schmitz (2008, n.p.) writes:

> Mass digitization and IRs fall on a single continuum of resources, yet they differ in many ways. Most notably, IRs provide scholars an opportunity to add to the body of recorded knowledge through publishing, while mass digitization makes a large existing corpus of printed literature available to scholars for use in their work.

Though the stream of scholarly output converges in the "digital middle," this conflation of content and format does not equate uniformity of approach. The institutional repository and mass-digitization project as exemplified by the MDL do not necessarily share the same approaches or values, despite that both are online digital platforms aimed at sharing content with users. Philosophies nevertheless diverge where digital formats might converge.

The decisions and policies for acquisition of materials changes and requires a new approach, such as sharing online content or subscription to materials. The model is altered for digital materials because of the issues regarding copyright, which had been developed over centuries through printing press culture.[10] In a short time the issues of copyright became complicated by the blurring of lines between copying, distributing, and disposing of digital content, which persists as a perfect copy (this issue is discussed in chapter 5). The current rights issues related to streaming truly redefine the digital library, especially those that include video, audio, and other multimedia formats.

With all these new approaches, the most fundamental service of the library, preservation, needs further solidification. New methods of digital storage and preservation are still being developed and must be tested over longer periods of time in order to start the process long-term accessibility and viability. The cloud storage services and LOCKSS initiatives that currently exist, including Amazon Glacier and MetaArchive, to name two currently popular choices, are still largely unproven. It remains to be seen whether they will survive longer-term shifts in the information technology landscape.

There is ever more reliance on portable electronics, systems, and networks. The smartphone and tablet have become important and ubiquitous information tools. Their quick adoption has altered how people approach the web and their digital libraries. Indeed, some universities are wholeheartedly adopting the mobile revolution with their own initiatives. California State University, Northridge, for example, implemented its myCSUNtablet initiative, which provides Apple iPad tablets to all students.[11] The iPad is provided at regular price, but the university funds new e-textbook development for the iPad that will create a "cost-neutral effect" for students.

Shifts in intellectual, organizational, and economic practices have occurred with digital libraries as well. End users' search behaviors have changed; people's reactions to information overload have been analyzed; organizations have become less centralized, and their services can occur in various locations; and new digital economies have shifted whole business models to meet the dominance of Facebook, Google, and other social media and web technologies, especially in the case of printing and publishing.

Looking at things through this lens, we can see that MDLs are more than just "larger" digital libraries of aggregated content. They have addressed and even solved many of the same problems as smaller digital libraries, but they have also developed a set of their own.

CHARACTERISTICS OF MDLS

If an MDL is more than just a supersized digital library, then what is it, exactly? What characteristics do we need to pin down to define one? Furthermore, why do we need to provide different nomenclature to describe it?

Thomas Kuhn (1970), in his groundbreaking work *The Structure of Scientific Revolutions*, discusses how scientific theories and concepts change over time. He argues that the change is neither a gradual one nor a progressive one. In many ways change in scientific models is revolutionary and therefore a complete alteration of everything people saw and experienced in the past. In his parlance this is a "paradigm shift." Though this terminology has been appropriated by business

21

jargon and has of late been applied inaccurately in popular discourse, the shift is an important way to conceptualize what is also occurring in information science.

Kuhn (1970, 110) writes:

> No paradigm ever solves all the problems it defines and . . . no two paradigms leave all the same problems unsolved. . . . Like the issue of competing standards, that question of values can be answered only in terms of criteria that lie outside of normal science altogether, and it is that recourse to external criteria that most obviously makes paradigm debates revolutionary.

In other words, scientific paradigms are by their very definition working models attempting to parse reality, yet at the same time they remain rule bound and are therefore able to pose and answer only questions that fall within the parameters of those rules.

To think outside of that framework is to court contradiction and confusion in the holder of the paradigm. As a result, paradigms often cannot overlap, and are often at cross-purposes, because they question different things and look for answers in different ways (Kuhn 1970).

In defining MDLs, taking a page from Kuhn's model, I have developed the following list of criteria and characteristics:

Collection size: Ranging from five hundred thousand to more than one million items

Acquisitions, collection development, and copyright concerns: Numerous partnering members contributing print book content that may or may not have copyright clearance

Content type: Mass-digitized print books or similar volume-centric holders of information (e.g., encyclopedias, atlases)

Collection diversity: Diversity dependent upon self-selected partnering members

Content access: Degrees of open access; single interfaces, such as search engines and portals, representing all the collections

Metadata: Gathered and aggregated from multiple sources, with a reliance on new schemas

Content and digital preservation: Large-scale preservation by consortium members

Collection Size

Scope

When defining something as an MDL, one important consideration is size. Generally, the massive digital library is one that has aggregated or gathered content from numerous sources into one web-defined area or domain. The largest MDLs work on a much grander scale. Google Books, for example, contains nearly thirty million books in its collection. HathiTrust, a consortium of several US-based and European universities, contains close to eleven million digital books, with 30 percent of those in the public domain. The numbers of materials at least partly accessible in MDLs range from the low hundreds of thousands of items (e.g., Internet Archive) to the tens of millions (e.g., HathiTrust, Google Books). Eventually, these will possibly reach hundred millions and more. In contrast, subject and institutional repositories are smaller in size. For example, MIT's DSpace repository, the pioneering institution of the DSpace software and IRs in general, contains only sixty-three thousand items, thirty-five thousand of which are electronic theses and dissertations. University of Kansas, another "top 100" institutional repository in the United States, houses only around ten thousand items.

Differentiating Issues

The sheer size of these collections raises issues that do not affect subject and institutional repositories or digital libraries and collections built on a smaller scale. Issues of findability and collection development become much more fraught with peril as subject and institutional repositories nonetheless remain small in scope and therefore more manageable. But what happens when collections get too large and need new approaches to confirm collection sizes? What if they are too big to fail, like the Wall Street banks of the 2008 recession? In this case "too big to fail" just means too big to hold accountable. In many ways the MDLs could be enamored of their own size. Other issues regarding size include the speed with which retrieval is possible and the increased amount of technological overhead needed to keep the project online and accessible.

Size is not in itself a good thing, either. The utility of a collection to its patrons matters more. Having access to the metadata records and full-text searching capability of some millions of books does, however, present a compelling benefit. WorldCat has a huge database of items, but it lacks the full-text searchability of Google Books.

WorldCat was developed in an era when it was considered "good enough" that a library catalog contained a few basic metadata elements, such as title, author, and subject heading. These ideas were based on what was possible to accomplish with a card catalog. MDLs like Google Books illuminate a new way forward in which we can dig into the content of the book, look at things like term frequencies, and rank the results list on the basis of those.

Acquisitions, Collection Development, and Copyright Law

Scope

The traditional model of library acquisition has been to purchase a book itself from a vendor or solicit the means to acquire books via donors. This worked in the print world quite well, with copyright laws providing the "exhaust rule" to allow libraries to accept, pass along, or dispose of books however they felt was appropriate. Libraries could band together quite easily and trade or lend books to users outside their main user base. Although digital versions of these materials are more easily shared and aggregated, current copyright law does not provide as much leeway for sharing these resources. Aggregation of content via multiple "online" partnering institutions results in some obstacles, especially if the traditional pillars of libraries, including fair use and section 108 of the Copyright Act, become weakened by such things as the Digital Millennium Copyright Act (DMCA) or a future full-scale revision.

In this regard, the MDL approaches content aggregation less like a smaller digital library and more like an online digital aggregator of journal and serial content. The resource type for the MDL is still generally the old-fashioned book, a technology perfected over the centuries after Gutenberg's press, but in a new digitally transformed format. The expression "new wine in old bottles" is almost inverted here, yet the new containers have the ability at times to transform the original content and add value to it, despite the movement from a three-dimensional type of media to a two-dimensional one. It is no secret that a digitized version of a master's thesis, for example, will receive new life in the digital milieu.

Differentiating Issues

In many ways the massive digital library is moving in tandem with the development of the so-called fourth paradigm—data-intensive research. The acquisition of the book is becoming less important than the large amounts of data and the large-scale trends that can be derived from former print-based cultures. Moving large data sets from print to digital, and moving large text sets, like a book to digital, opens up amazing possibilities for the mining of data, not only in the sciences but also in the humanities. One can search, for example, the frequency that terms appear in the Google Books corpus and track those through data visualizations over time. HathiTrust has a similar search as well. The smaller-scale digital library does not have such a robust capability for data mining.

Smaller digital libraries have also focused generally on the content that exists within their physical holdings, though with some creating limited consortia to distribute digital content—mostly archival materials, university publications (e.g., yearbooks), and other generally public domain materials. However, MDLs have established partnerships to increase the totals of their online digital-print collections, but at the risk of stretching the boundaries of ownership and acquisition. While this works for offline content, since copyright law allows it, copyright law does not explicitly support sharing copies online.

The model of aggregation works well enough for journals and article databases since the publishers themselves have developed the content. However, licensed material comes at an expensive cost to libraries and increases yearly. It may be that MDLs will eventually have to abandon open access and move to pricing models to be sustainable and to avoid legal entanglements.

25

Collection Content

Scope

Currently, the exemplars of the MDL field focus purely on the mass-digitized book or similar volume-centric collections of print materials. Generally, the books come from various MDL partnerships, including universities and large public libraries across the United States. Google Books, for example, digitizes the books from about twenty to twenty-five academic and public library collections from across the United States and internationally. A large amount of the books digitized are in the public domain and help users unable to access special collections or archives at institutions.

Differentiating Issues

In many ways MDLs should be able to expand their content types very quickly. Instead of relying purely on the digitized print book collections, some will move into the areas of audio; video; and alternative publications, such as atlases, musical scores, and the like. Some MDLs already focus some of their collections on materials such as web resources or multimedia digital files (e.g., Internet Archive's Wayback Machine and Grateful Dead bootlegged concert recordings). It may be possible in the future that updated editions in e-book format or new born-digital e-books may replace or complicate the accessibility of some of the works currently residing within the MDLs.

Collection Diversity

Scope

Similar to the parameter of collection size, the diversity found in MDL collections is significantly broader and deeper than the typical digital library collection or institutional repository. This is largely a reflection of the aggregation of multiple partners. Diversity has the potential to be greater than any other type of digital library, yet it could still be less than that of a research I–level university academic library or large public library's print collection.

Differentiating Issues

With just a fraction of collections currently digitized and available online and the general primacy of the English language in the main MDLs based in the United States, prioritization of limited resources set aside for digitization projects tends to favor English-language materials. With this emphasis, collection diversity is compromised. Factors such as MDL aggregator partnerships and language-primacy policies of such libraries become paramount considerations. If an MDL partners with foreign universities (as in the case of Google with Keio University or HathiTrust with Biblioteca de la Universidad Complutense de Madrid), the likelihood of broader and deeper diversity increases. But as is discussed in chapter 7, there are still flaws in this approach. Nevertheless, MDLs are notable in comparison to their small digital library counterparts for their ability to increase diversity in subject-matter representation.

Content Access

Scope

Although single search interfaces are nothing new to digital libraries, often the implication with a small digital library or digital asset management system's series of collections (e.g., a CONTENTdm collection), is that the items are generally available in the same locations, or at least the materials have some physical or locational ties. Provenance in this sense becomes an important defining characteristic of the library and its "new and improved" digital version.

Digital libraries already test the bounds of physical provenance, with many of them aggregating collections on a minor scale. However, with MDLs the sense of physical location is rendered nearly irrelevant. The point of the MDL becomes not adding value to a physical collection that will nonetheless remain tied together (and continue to be meaningful as a physical collection), but obliterating and recombining collections into something malleable and new. The importance of access trumps the need to completely preserve physical provenance.

Along with erasing the existing boundaries, MDLs also provide at least some amount of open access material, especially with books that have fallen into the public domain. As a result, some issues pertaining to open access to copyrighted and orphan works arise.

Differentiating Issues

MDLs can remove the barriers between systems, but they can also hide the originating sources. Sometimes, then, the contextual meanings derived from a collection of materials can be lost, though this is arguably more a concern with archives, which function on the principle of provenance. At the same time, meaning need not necessarily be derived from context. This frees users to recombine knowledge by surpassing the boundaries of subject fields, classifications, and taxonomies.

Open access becomes a moral imperative when dealing with public domain books. Many of the works digitized by all MDLs are openly accessible, but errors and mistakes have been found in studies of Google Books by the authors (James and Weiss 2012). Orphan works by far represent the thorniest of all the problems related to digitized book content. Publishers need to revisit some of their policies. As researcher Paul J. Heald shows, there is a huge gap in the amount of books available between the 1930s and 1990s.[12] Almost sixty years are missing in disproportionate amounts. MDLs might help alleviate this issue.

Metadata Development

Scope

The MARC record has long been the defining metadata standard for print matter, especially books. In fact, no other metadata is as robust or as finely tuned to the needs of libraries and their printed shelf matter. However, as print formats give way to digital media, the MARC record has not been meeting many of the needs of the digital age. As a result, digital libraries and collections are moving toward metadata schemas more appropriate for digital materials. In particular, the Dublin Core metadata schema has been adopted almost universally for digital collections. Some MDLs are able to aggregate and crosswalk, which consists of mapping similar elements to each other, numerous metadata schemas. This is an important defining feature: the ability to crosswalk multiple metadata to aggregate immense data in its systems. Many systems already are able to do this, including repositories compliant with the Open Archive Initiative's Protocol for Metadata Harvesting.

Differentiating Issues

One of the biggest problems with digital copies is the possibility of losing the tie with the physical object. Without metadata available to anchor a digital version to the original object, it could quite literally and figuratively be "lost at sea." MDLs have shown issues with incorporating metadata from various siloed institutions. The crosswalking of aggregated data becomes a major issue when mistakes from the source collections appear. The aggregation is only as good as the source material. How does an MDL, then, deal with metadata quality control? How would an MDL begin to approach such important issues related to metadata and interoperability?

Digital Content Preservation

Scope

One of the main reasons given for digitizing content has been the creation of digital copies that would provide stand in for the original version. Digitization is therefore implemented as a protective measure. Digital preservation as a practice includes refresh, migration, replication, emulation, encapsulation, the concept of persistent archives, and metadata attachment. Digital libraries have attempted to incorporate these practices into their sustainable frameworks and to follow specific guidelines set up by various organizations. The philosophy of long-term preservation of digital content has been one of the guiding principles for the creation of most online digital collections.

Differentiating Issues

In reality, true digital preservation has proved to be elusive. Not all digital libraries exist as preservation platforms. Those that have preservation policies are sometimes unable to follow through because of increased costs or insufficient funding. Some larger initiatives like Microsoft's Live Search Books and Live Search Academic have been abandoned.[13] In small-scale digital collections, issues of digital collection preservation have generally been developed and regulated effectively. Several organizations, including DRAMBORA, Trac, Nestor, and Platter, provide specific guidelines for offering a trusted digital collection.

However, MDLs have also been at the forefront in developing digital preservation methodologies. HathiTrust, in particular, has taken the lead on this. Internet archive and Open Content Alliance have embraced this as part of their missions as well. Issues of digital preservation will need to address scalability and feasibility. It may be necessary for those involved with MDLs to create new procedures for handling the preservation of digital copies of print books.

One unintended problem with the practice of digital preservation is that ultimately some meaning is still lost in the transference from one format to another. Scholars and historians can derive as much from the context and physical materials of a book (e.g., marginalia, binding) as from the written content. On a large scale, such loss of material could be devastating. In chapter 13 this issue is central to the problem of digitizing Japanese-language books. Imagine if scholars were unable to look at the ads in newspapers because the aggregator had excised them from their database—leaving only the text of the article. Much would be lost. In this case, some guidelines on digital preservation of books should be examined with relationship to MDLs.

CONCLUSION

In summary, these criteria and their attendant issues, though entirely unique to the digital library, may require different approaches when dealing with a massive digital library. The issues involved with aggregating millions of decentralized, previously published print materials into one uniform conceptual space become more complex. It is important to differentiate, therefore, between smaller counterparts, as they are easier to police and analyze than MDLs, especially with regard to metadata uniformity, copyright compliance, and ownership. The larger the institution or system, the more unwieldy and slow to change it may become. As seen earlier, the issues are not entirely a matter of amplification or magnification of a regular-sized digital library.

Furthermore, some institutions deemed "too big to fail" may underperform if users and critics are not vigilant. In the case of corporations and businesses, the market is often determined to be the appropriate judge of an organization success. Efficiency in operations may be important for the bottom lines of for-profit organizations, including for-profit universities, corporate-owned massive open online courses (MOOCs), and traditional publishers. However, in dealing with consortia of public and nonprofit educational institutions, market forces should not be the sole factor determining their overall sustainability, especially when the content is of significant cultural and social value. It is in this vein that a series of criteria for evaluating and classifying the MDL becomes important for helping to preserve and protect long-term access and sustainability.

REFERENCES

Fox, Edward, Robert Akscyn, Richard Furuta, and John Leggett. 1995. "Digital Libraries." *Communications of the ACM* 38, no. 4: 22–28.

Hahn, Trudi Bellardo. 2008. "Mass Digitization: Implications for Preserving the Scholarly Record." *Library Resources and Technical Services* 52, no. 1: 18–26.

Ishizuka, Kathy. 2005. "Showing Google the Way." *School Library Journal* 51, no. 2: 26–27.

James, Ryan, and Andrew Weiss. 2012. "An Assessment of Google Books' Metadata." *Journal of Library Metadata* 12, no. 1: 15–22.

Jeanneney, Jean-Noël. 2007. *Google and the Myth of Universal Knowledge. A View from Europe*. Chicago: University of Chicago Press. First published in French in 2005.

Kuhn, Thomas S. 1970. *The Structure of Scientific Revolutions*. 2nd ed. Chicago: University of Chicago Press.

Licklider, J. C. R. 1965. *Libraries of the Future*. Cambridge, MA: MIT Press.

Schmitz, Dawn. 2008. *The Seamless Cyberinfrastructure: The Challenges of Studying Users of Mass Digitization and Institutional Repositories*. Washington, DC: Council on Library and Information Resources. www.clir.org/pubs/archives/schmitz.pdf.

Venkatraman, Archana. 2009. "Europe Must Seize Lead on Digital Books, Urges Reading." *Information World Review*, no. 260: 1-1.

Weiss, Andrew, and Ryan James. 2013a. "Assessing the Coverage of Hawaiian and Pacific Books in the Google Books Digitization Project." *OCLC Systems and Services* 29, no. 1: 13–21.

Weiss, Andrew, and Ryan James. 2013b. "An Examination of Massive Digital Libraries' Coverage of Spanish Language Materials: Issues of Multi-Lingual Accessibility in a Decentralized, Mass-Digitized World." Paper presented at the International Conference on Culture and Computing, Ritsumeikan University, Kyoto, Japan, September 16.

NOTES

1. See the website for Google Books Library Project, at www.google.com/googlebooks/library/.

2. Lanier, quoted in Scott Timberg, "Jaron Lanier: The Internet Destroyed the Middle Class," *Salon,* May 12, 2013, www.salon.com/2013/05/12/jaron_lanier_the_internet_destroyed_the_middle_class/.

3. John P. Wilkin, University of Michigan, quoted at "Library Partners," Google Books, http://books.google.com/googlebooks/library/partners.html.

4. "Workshop Objectives," Fourth Workshop on Very Large Digital Libraries, September 29, 2011, www.delos.info/vldl2011/.

5. Ibid.

6. Ibid.

7. Giuseppe Amato, "Dealing with Very Large Visual Document Archives," presentation at the Fourth Workshop on Very Large Digital Libraries, September 29, 2011, www.delos.info/vldl2011/program/1.VLDL2011.pdf.

8. "Workshop Objectives," Fourth Workshop on Very Large Digital Libraries, September 29, 2011, www.delos.info/vldl2011/.

9. See the American Memory project website, at http://memory.loc.gov/ammem/index.html.

10. "Copyright Timeline," Association of Research Libraries, www.arl.org/focus-areas/copyright-ip/2486-copyright-timeline.

11. "myCSUNtablet initiative," California State University, Northridge, April 5, 2013, www.csun.edu/it/news/ipad-initiative.

12. Rebecca Rosen, "The Hole in Our Collective Memory: How Copyright Made Mid-Century Books Vanish," *Atlantic,* July 30, 2013, www.theatlantic.com/technology/archive/2013/07/the-hole-in-our-collective-memory-how-copyright-made-mid-century-books-vanish/278209/.

13. Michael Arrington, "Microsoft to Shut Live Search Books," TechCrunch, May 23, 2008, http://techcrunch.com/2008/05/23/microsoft-to-shut-live-search-books/.

Chapter Three

Major Players and Their Characteristics— or, Who's at the Party?

EXEMPLAR MASSIVE DIGITAL LIBRARIES

Despite the long gestation period in the development of digital systems from the 1960s to their uniform application across all libraries by the late 1990s and early 2000s, the creation and development of massive digital libraries (MDLs) almost seems to have occurred overnight in the mid-2000s. Google's announcement in 2004 that it would join the fray by digitizing all the world's books seems to have galvanized a number of already-existing projects and to have spawned a few more. Several MDL projects developed simultaneously over the past decade and have become the leading exemplars of the movement toward larger aggregated collections of digitized print material.

Interestingly, many of these MDLs comprise partners that overlap with other MDLs. As a result, many of the projects can provide similar accessibility to online content. Books digitized by the Google Books Library Project, for example, appear in HathiTrust, Internet Archive, and the Open Content Alliance. An exact number is not forthcoming, however.

The following looks at these major players among MDLs and briefly examines their characteristics. The list is by no means exhaustive, but it should allow readers to get a better sense of how the major MDLs stack up against one another. Criteria described for each MDL include their dates of inception, modi operandi, the estimated size of the collections, the subjects collected, the number of partner institutions, the languages covered in the collections, and so on. The Alexa ranking included in the list of descriptors provides a general metric allowing evaluators to assess the amount of users and site traffic.

This chapter examines the following MDLs: Google Books, HathiTrust, Internet Archive, the Open Content Alliance's Open Library, the Library of Congress's American Memory, the Networked Digital Library of Theses and Dissertations, the Virtual Library of Historical Newspapers, the European Commission's digital libraries initiative, and France's Gallica. The MDLs are discussed in general order of collection size and split between US-based MDLs, European-based MDLs, and MDLs of special note.

CURRENT US-BASED MDLS

Google Books

Fact Sheet

- Starting date: 2004
- Modus operandi: "To create a comprehensive, searchable, virtual card catalog"
- Size: 30 million volumes
- Subjects or scope: All
- Partner institutions: 20–25 estimated
- Languages: English primarily, but many other languages as well; breakdowns are undetermined (request from Google for breakdowns was not honored)
- URL: http://books.google.com/
- Accessibility: Snippet, partial view and full view
- Digital collection development policy: "Digitize the whole of the world's 129,864,880 books"
- Alexa ranking: No. 1 in the world (April 2014)

The Google Books (see figure 3.1) project started in 2004. It currently holds about fifteen million volumes in its collections. Sergei Brin, a founder of Google and co-inventor of its revolutionary search engine, envisioned Google Books as a replacement for the library card catalog. This effectively threw down the gauntlet against a number of institutions, including national cultural institutions, public and academic libraries, and the publishing industry. The number 129,864,880 listed

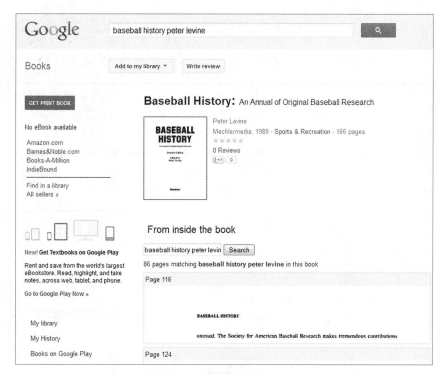

FIGURE 3.1

Snippet view of Google Books' display of Baseball History, by Peter Levine.
Metadata provided next to the thumbnail image of the book's cover
and at the bottom of the page (not shown).

in the Google Books fact sheet is significant in that a software engineer working on the Google Books project estimated this figure.[1]

Google Books is characterized in part by its extremely robust and flexible search engine. When searching in this MDL, a large amount of set results often appear. Mistakes in the search are often autocorrected. Google's stated goal is the digitization of all the books in the world, a number that reaches about 120 million. The project works with about twenty public and academic institutions in several countries, including Japan, Germany, England, and Spain. Overall collection diversity is present, with a large number of languages represented and accessible, although most materials in the corpus are in the English language.

The Google Books corpus is open to anyone able to use a computer that is connected to the Internet. However, because of copyright restrictions and the threat of litigation, any materials not within the public domain have been closed to full-text viewing. Google allows users three levels of accessibility to the texts beyond the metadata record: "snippet view," which is a few sentences of the book; "partial view," which is often several to dozens of pages; and "full view," which is the complete text.

One issue that arises with the functionality of Google Books, however, is the inability of the search engine to accurately retrieve and coherently display single works of multiple volumes. A search, for example, of the Harvard Classics—a fifty-one-volume series—results in a very jumbled retrieval. Unless a user knew beforehand that the Harvard Classics series contained fifty-one volumes, he or she might never get an accurate accounting from Google's set result.

HathiTrust

Fact Sheet

- Starting date: 2008
- Modus operandi: "Contribute to the common good by collecting, organizing, preserving, communicating, and sharing the record of human knowledge"
- Size: 11 million volumes (approximately 3 million in public domain)
- Subjects or scope: University academic library subject matter
- Partner institutions: approximately 72 research libraries
- Languages: 429 languages—48% English, 9% German, 7% French, 4.5% Spanish, 4% Chinese, 3.7% Russian, 3% Japanese
- URL: www.hathitrust.org
- Accessibility: Limited view with full-text search results only and full view
- Digital collection development policy: "Build a comprehensive archive of published literature from around the world and develop shared strategies for managing and developing their digital and print holdings in a collaborative way"
- Alexa ranking: No. 53,758 (April 2014)

HathiTrust (see figure 3.2) started in 2008. It currently holds about eleven million volumes in its collections. HathiTrust's essential mission is to meet the needs of the members of its partnering institutions. Collection development is focused on gathering digitized books and journals from partner institutions and in-house digital initiatives and those books digitized in part by Google Books and the Internet Archive. The partners include nearly seventy-two world-class academic research

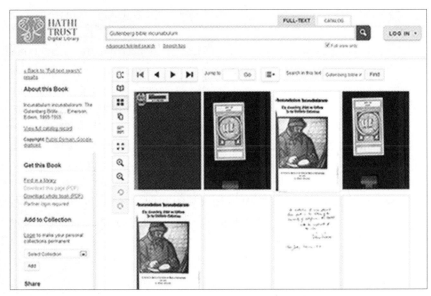

FIGURE 3.2
Full view of thumbnails in the HathiTrust of Miguel Cervantes'
Don Quixote de la Mancha, London, J. J. Dubochet, 1837–39.
Translated from the Spanish, v. 1. Cervantes Saavedra,
Miguel de, 1547–1616. (public domain book).

and national libraries. Notable partners include the Library of Congress and the California Digital Library.

As one might expect, English is the main language of the archive. Nearly three million books, representing 48 percent of holdings, are in English. The second-largest represented group is German, followed by French, Spanish, Chinese, Russian, and Japanese. Given the large Spanish-speaking population in the United States, the small amount of Spanish-language materials is surprising. However, given that the audience is college students and faculty, German and French have long represented the frontiers of scholarship in more disciplines than Spanish has.

HathiTrust is characterized by a robust search engine and extremely well-organized metadata and records management. Where Google Books has issues with the retrieval of specific dates and other types of metadata, HathiTrust performs information retrieval and document display with superior results. The system allows, however, only two types of views to users who are not members: a limited view, which allows only search results to retrieve word counts for queries (i.e., full-text search), and full view, which is reserved for materials in the public domain.

Access is open to anyone able to use a computer connected to the Internet, but partnering institutions and their members can benefit from extra services, such as content storage, data preservation, and copyright clearance and usage consultation. Although the current size of the collection is smaller than that of Google Books, the ability to find information more easily should make the HathiTrust the go-to MDL for libraries.

Another positive aspect is the manner in which HathiTrust handles multivolume works. Compared to the mish-mash one gets from a Google Books search result for multiple-volume works—the Harvard Classics, for example—HathiTrust generally keeps these volumes bundled together in a record. The user can then easily find and access all volumes together.

Open Content Alliance

Fact Sheet

- Starting date: 2005
- Modus operandi: "A collaborative effort of a group of cultural, technology, nonprofit, and governmental organizations from around the world that helps build a permanent archive of multilingual digitized text and multimedia material"
- Size: 2,654,228 works; 23 million book records in Open Library beta
- Subjects or scope: Public library, government, and individual international authors
- Partner institutions: Initially: Yahoo!, Internet Archive, Microsoft, University of California, and University of Toronto—currently approximately 2,300 individual organizations (in several consortia)
- Languages: Primarily English, with a large amount of Spanish, Japanese, and other languages. Full breakdowns unknown.
- URL: www.opencontentalliance.org
- Accessibility: Full view or a record; log-in for members to check out books; DAISY-standard compliant digital files for visually impaired users, including the blind and dyslexic (DAISY Consortium)

FIGURE 3.3
OCA metadata for Don Quijote translated into German.

- Digital collection development policy: "One web page for every book," and to provide books for people with visual impairments and/or disabilities
- Alexa ranking: No. 1,542,664 (April 2014)

The Open Content Alliance's (OCA) Open Library (see figure 3.3) started as a counterpoint to Google Books, with Yahoo!, Internet Archive, and University of California joining to create the initiative. Microsoft joined the mass-digitization movement with its own digitization project, Live Book Search, in 2005 but dropped out by 2008 after having scanned roughly 750,000 books. One of the priorities of Open Library is accessibility for people who are blind and/or have disabilities, such as dyslexia, with its reliance on the Digital Accessible Information System (DAISY) technology.

Open Library has also positioned itself as an alternative to WorldCat, by championing its service as a "web page for every book." The site provides information about most books and provides readable book image files for users. Members can also borrow the physical books and access other books that at-large public users may not.

Internet Archive

Fact Sheet

- Starting date: 1996
- Modus operandi: "Universal access to all knowledge"
- Size: 10 million web pages: 1.6 million volumes and 23 million book records (as a result of partnering and/or sponsoring the Open Library project with OCA)
- Subjects or scope: Combination of media (audio and video), books, and web pages—archives using Wayback Machine
- Partner institutions: OCA, Smithsonian, Library of Congress, and more; includes access to the online initiatives of Universal Library, Project Gutenberg, Children's Library, Biodiversity Heritage Library, and more
- Languages: English primarily, Spanish, and more; full breakdowns unknown
- URL: http://archive.org
- Accessibility: All items included are open access and public domain, so no restrictions in access
- Digital collection development policy: "Change the content of the Internet from ephemera to enduring artifacts of our political and cultural lives"
- Alexa ranking: No. 159 (April 2014)

The Internet Archive (see figure 3.4) is a unique addition to the MDL category. On the one hand, its main focus appears to be archiving the Internet via its Wayback Machine. One of its stated goals, in fact, is to create archival artifacts of the web itself. This is important, as the Internet may replace many print media sources that are available, including books. On the other hand, its primary concern has been less on the number of titles acquired than do Google Books, HathiTrust, and even the OCA, which focus heavily on collection sizes. Instead, the Internet Archive gathers and approves only those materials in the public domain or that have author permissions. As a result, its print-derived digital collections are smaller but completely accessible.

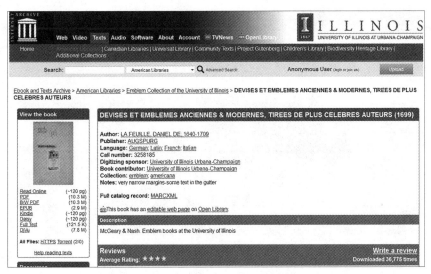

FIGURE 3.4
View of screenshot showing Internet Archive's display
of *Devises et emblemes anciennes and modernes,* 1699.

An advantage of the Internet Archive is also that it provides links to several mass-digitization projects and allows the projects to exist under their own names, as well as within the Internet Archive web pages. Projects such as the Biodiversity Heritage Library, Project Gutenberg, the Universal Library, and Children's Library are worthy open access book digitization initiatives aimed at providing people with free access to resources, which falls under the Internet Archive umbrella.

A difference of Internet Archive is one of scope, with its emphasis on video and audio, especially in relation to its well-known Grateful Dead Collection of the band's legendary live recordings. Additionally, Internet Archive also provides access to about 9,500 audio recordings of books, including literature and poetry.

EUROPEAN-BASED MDLS OF NOTE

Europeana

Fact Sheet

- Starting date: 2008
- Modus operandi: Meta-aggregator and display space for European digitized works

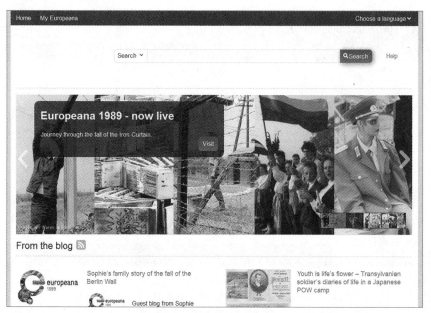

FIGURE 3.5
Screenshot showing the home page of the Europeana Digital Library.

- Size: 10 million objects, almost 4.3 million volumes of texts and books (more than 350,000 in English)
- Subjects or scope: European culture
- Partner institutions: Roughly 130 institutions, including universities, museums, and organizations across Europe
- Languages: Full range of European languages, including English, Slavic, and Basque
- URL: www.europeana.eu/portal/
- Accessibility: Items available as open access, restricted and behind pay-walls
- Digital collection development policy: Very strong application of public domain rights; "the Europeana Foundation believe in and wish to strengthen the concept of the Public Domain in the digitised world"
- Alexa ranking: No. 44,296 (April 2014)

The Europeana digital library (see figure 3.5) aggregates content from more than 130 institutions across Europe. As a result, it is a fully multilingual, multicultural endeavor. There appears not to be one dominant language in the project. With a huge collection of more than four million texts, the digital library should be considered a leading MDL in the field. Its emphasis on interoperability and a strong metadata schema allows users to refine searches and hone in on more relevant search results easily. The main focus for the library is to ensure that digital materials of numerous cultures remain freely accessible to all. The project advocates the strongest pro–public domain stance of nearly all the MDLs. It is a vital and important MDL as a result.

Gallica

Fact Sheet

- Starting date: 1997
- Modus operandi: "Collective digital library"
- Size: 2.5 million documents—460,000 books and 36,145 manuscripts
- Subjects or scope: —
- Partner institutions: Mainly French libraries, museums, and universities, but also the Library of Congress and the National Library of Brazil
- Languages: Primarily French, but other languages on a small scale, including English, Spanish, Portuguese, and German
- URL: http://gallica.bnf.fr; English-language URL: http://gallica.bnf.fr/?lang=EN
- Accessibility: Many resources are open access; provide permanent links to items
- Digital collection development policy: Unknown
- Alexa ranking: No. 13,641 (April 2014)

Gallica, supported by the Bibliothèque Nationale de France (see figure 3.6) despite its relatively smaller book collection size, is noteworthy for several reasons. First, it is an MDL primarily focused on France and Francophone works. Its partners include many universities and museums in France, but also the National Library of Brazil and the Library of Congress. There are some books offered in English, but these are few compared to other MDLs and are dwarfed, obviously, by the size of the French-language collection. Gallica is also, in many ways, an MDL counterpoint to Google Books, with a very different philosophy and approach to the digital library.

FIGURE 3.6
Screenshot showing the home page
for Bibliothèque Nationale de France's Gallica.

Virtual Library of Historical Newspapers

Fact Sheet

- Starting date: 2006
- Modus operandi: "To search for any word on any page of any digital newspaper"
- Size: 1,049,943 issues, from 2,037 serials
- Subjects or scope: Spanish-language newspapers and serials from the Iberian Peninsula
- Partner institutions: 18 autonomous regions of Spain, 57 provinces (subdivisions of the autonomous regions), and 180 towns
- Languages: Primarily Spanish

FIGURE 3.7
Screenshot showing the home page
for the Virtual Library of Historical Newspapers.

- URL: http://prensahistorica.mcu.es/en/consulta/busqueda.cmd
- Accessibility: Open access for 5 million pages of newspapers
- Digital collection development policy: To preserve bibliographic materials that are in danger of disappearing because of their physical characteristics and to disseminate more broadly information resources that are widely used by researchers and citizens in general
- Alexa ranking: No. 29,466 (April 2014)

The Virtual Library of Historical Newspapers (VLHN) (see figure 3.7) focuses on Spanish-language newspapers and serials. Nearly five million pages are available through OCR full-text search. Many of the regions of Spain and its provinces and towns are represented by the library. Explanatory information is available in English, but the MDL is mainly Spanish in its focus. It is meant to provide access to fragile and rare serial materials, and it allows users to access the information without risking damage or loss to the original materials. In contrast to many other digital newspaper aggregators, the project is providing the papers in an openly accessible manner.

MDLS OF SPECIAL NOTE

Networked Digital Library of Theses and Dissertations

Fact Sheet

- Starting date: 1996
- Modus operandi: "Promotes the adoption, creation, use, dissemination and preservation of electronic theses and dissertations"
- Size: 2,400,000 (or more) records
- Subjects or scope: Electronic theses and dissertations from all academic subjects
- Partner institutions: 91 institutional members (mostly universities) and three well-known consortia: OhioLINK, Florida Consortium, and Triangle Research Libraries Network
- Languages: Primarily English; full breakdowns unknown
- URL: www.ndltd.org
- Accessibility: Varies—some ETDs are publicly available, but many are behind access walls or embargoed
- Digital collection development policy: limited only to ETDs; the MDL wants to partner with as many ETD-creating organizations as possible
- Alexa ranking: No. 1,014,425 (April 2014)

The Networked Digital Library of Theses and Dissertations (NDLTD) (see figure 3.8) began in the mid-1990s to promote the creation and accessibility of electronic theses and dissertations (ETDs). It is a robust system that allows users to search across numerous repositories and digital libraries to access ETDs. For the most part, the language most represented in the collection is English, especially as most member institutions are based in the United States.

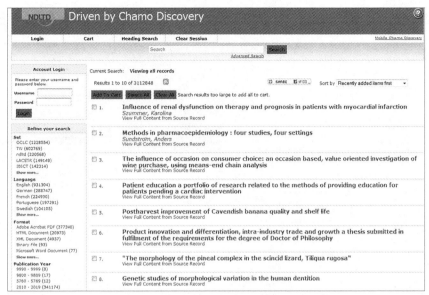

FIGURE 3.8
Screenshot of NDLTD home page showing
the first 10 of 3.112 million records.

Accessibility is a main issue for ETDs. They are somewhat of an outlier in terms of the publishing world—part publication, part archiving. Since a large majority of traditional publishers do not consider a thesis or dissertation placed online as a typical publication, accessibility should not be an issue. However, many students and scholars still fear not being able to publish their thesis if it appears already online. Embargoes therefore have become an issue with ETDs. Yet most publishers will also rarely publish a thesis or dissertation without major revisions and edits, essentially rendering moot the embargo protection. Though most of the organizations allied with the NDLTD advocate open access, the reality remains that many still limit access to content.

American Memory—Library of Congress

Fact Sheet

- Starting date: pilot 1990–94, launch 1996
- Modus operandi: "Be a gateway to the Library of Congress's vast resources of digitized American historical materials. Comprising more than 9 million items that document U.S. history and culture"

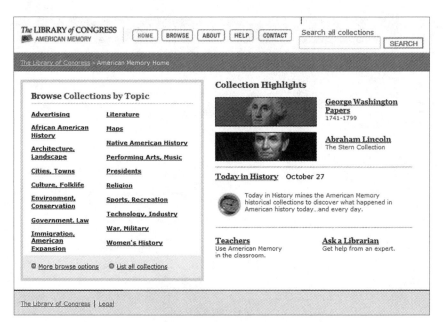

FIGURE 3.9
Screenshot of the Library of Congress's
American Memory project.

- Size: 9 million items total, including films, maps, and images; number of books is unknown
- Subjects or scope: American history and American archival materials
- Partner institutions: None
- Languages: Primarily English
- URL: http://memory.loc.gov/ammem/index.html
- Accessibility: US government works are in the public domain
- Digital collection development policy: Only a small fraction of collection is digitized; the focus is on digitizing the library's "unique holdings" and "exceptional primary sources"
- Alexa ranking: No. 4,366

The Library of Congress's American Memory (see figure 3.9) project is probably one of the pioneering digital libraries not only in the United States but also in the world. Many of the works in the Library of Congress are of great historical interest. Digital versions of the Declaration of Independence, the Constitution, and other early documents are available through this site. Early texts are also available. The focus of this MDL, then, is more of historical and public domain materials related to the American experience. The size of the MDL's books collection is undetermined at this time. Queries to the Library of Congress were successful, but specific numbers regarding the amount of books in the project were not provided in correspondence. The reference librarian for the Library of Congress wrote:

> Items in American Memory have item records that correlate one-to-one and one-to-many with files. For example, some books have a single image file for each page and some have three (GIF, JPEG, TIFF) for each page. Some also have SGML and on-the-fly HTML text transcriptions, as well. Some have only transcriptions; some have transcriptions with images only for illustrated pages. (Personal communication, reference specialist, Digital Reference Section, Library of Congress, July 25, 2013)

As a result, it appears quite difficult to determine the exact number of books in the American Memory project.

CONCLUSION

The various MDLs covered in this chapter show striking individuality in their approaches to mass digitization and the mass distribution of digitized content. Their central missions, to share the content of print books that may be locked away on bookshelves, are admirable. Varying degrees of scope, subject matter, and audience shape the massive collections in individual ways, making each MDL unique. Overall, when looking at the main examples of MDLs currently in existence, one gets the sense that ambitions for a unified digital front for all types of materials is the impetus driving their development. Some of the implications for this have impacts, as readers will see in the next chapter, on bricks-and-mortar libraries, which may have to scramble to accommodate as well as take advantage of these new initiatives.

NOTE

1. Joab Jackson, "Google: 129 Million Different Books Have Been Published," *PC World*, August 6, 2010, www.pcworld.com/article/202803/google_129_million_different _books_have_been_published.html.

Chapter Four

Impact on Librarianship—or, How Do I Deal with This?

Now that the characteristics of massive digital libraries have been clearly delineated in Chapter 2 and their main exemplars outlined in Chapter 3, we arrive at some important questions. First, how will libraries come to deal with MDLs? How will MDLs affect librarians and librarianship? How will they be examined and analyzed from an information science perspective?

When Jeanneney (2007) staked his position against Google, he was pointing out what he saw as proprietary interests overtaking the traditional cornerstones of both culture and academia. In many ways, Jeanneney's suspicions were not entirely unwarranted. As we will see in Chapter 5, the dispute with Google regarding the need to gain copyright permission to digitally index the entire corpus of the extant books still remains controversial. Jeanneney also predicted some dire consequences that have yet to come to pass. In time, though, the initially jarring presence of MDLs has given way to more reasoned acceptance. Some parties may now even see the benefit of these tools.

At the same time, MDLs are not limited merely to Google Books. Other massive digital libraries have been established that provide very different organizational philosophies and policies. HathiTrust, Internet Archive, Open Content Alliance, Europeana, and Gallica provide some of the same content, though on slightly smaller scales, but without the influence of shareholders and profiteering.

As for future impact, the answer is difficult to come by. First, it is difficult to pin down which problems will arise in the future and which current ones will either be resolved or worsen. The train may be coming, but it's difficult to always know

Ryan James contributed to this chapter.

51

if and when it will cross our path. Many predictions have failed to occur, making prognosticators look foolish at best.

However, certain broad trends are obvious. The major impacts of the past twenty years are here to stay for the immediate and midrange future, including the rise of ubiquitous high-speed Internet, the development of mobile technology, and the development of open access web publishing as an alternative to traditional publishers. MDLs are no different in their potential for long-term impact on libraries.

The traditional library has always offered an array of typical services, including access to print books, for those just-in-case uses; access to online digital works behind paywalls; access to old and rare materials; provision of study spaces, and increasingly quiet and collaborative (though some would say loud) study areas; provision of interlibrary loan (ILL) materials; preservation of print and digital assets; and collection shaping to meet the needs of perceived immediate user groups, cohorts, and stakeholders.

This chapter looks at some of these traditional roles of libraries and offers some ideas on how, philosophically and practically, MDLs might influence them in positive and negative ways.

ACCESS TO PRINT BOOKS

First and foremost, patrons primarily associate the library with access to print media, especially books, magazines, newspapers, and maps. In this regard MDLs may appear to have the greatest impact. MDLs have taken as their philosophies the digitization and provision of access to print books as they have traditionally been defined over the centuries: a bound collection of a single work or series of works in multiple volumes. Yet currently the models for MDLs have mostly been indiscriminate about their collection development, focusing purely on the traditional book model but in a digitally replicated form. Essentially, monographs, fiction, nonfiction, and the like, exist as facsimile copies with the added value of full-text searchability.

Yet other print materials associated with libraries are not well represented or approached by MDLs uniformly. Maps, atlases, newspapers, and magazines have all been underrepresented or ignored among the major MDLs. With the primacy of the monograph book in MDLs, much content remains outside their spheres of influence. A notable exception appears to be Google Books' inclusion of *Life* magazine in its corpus. If a large amount of magazines were represented in the

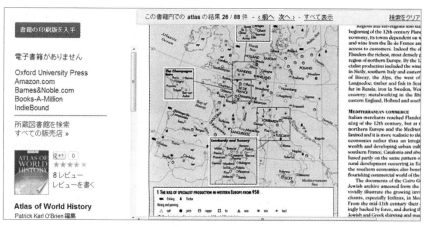

FIGURE 4.1

Screenshot of a map in the *Atlas of World History*, by Patrick Karl O'Brien, as it appears in the Google Books viewer, showing insufficient image resolution for detailed examination.

corpus, this might have an impact on libraries. Yet again, the number of possible magazines and the amount published over the past hundred years may prevent this.

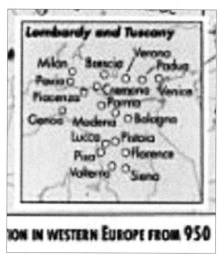

FIGURE 4.2

Detail of *Atlas of World History*, by Patrick Karl O'Brien, as it appears in the Google Books viewer, showing insufficient image resolution at high magnification.

Although some MDL projects, like the Spanish-language Virtual Library of Historical Newspapers, include newsprint, the sheer volume of these works may prevent MDLs from developing viable collections around them. As for atlases, image resolution and visibility currently impede the readability of oversize maps or atlases with maps printed across two pages. As book pages are rendered in the Google Books viewer as they are in print, some issues of pixelation can appear in maps. While text may be visible, the details in the image are not.

In figures 4.1 and 4.2, taken from Google Books, for example, a map in the seventh edition of *Essential World Atlas*, pixelates under magnification and displays on its side. The page cannot be rotated and as a result is almost useless to a typical user. This shows the difficulty that mass digitization may have in presenting non-text-focused books. Additionally, the large sizes of atlases and their often irregular shapes—some can be square, for example—may slow down mass digitization projects.

In summary, better access to print works in MDLs is likely to remain limited to monographs for some time. The specialty print items like atlases that resist large-scale efficient digitization projects may require more care in digitization efforts. Ultimately, should there be an interest or need for it, libraries might consider working to digitize these works locally over time until the time is right for the federation of such large collections.

ACCESS TO OLD AND RARE MATERIALS

Access to old and rare materials is likely the greatest positive benefit that MDLs might confer upon libraries and their users. People would surely be able to access materials that were hidden or protected from the general public. A great example of this is the Vatican Library's attempt to digitize forty million pages of the nearly eighty-two thousand ancient manuscripts held in its collection. Although slightly smaller in scope than the largest MDLs, the project provides a glimpse into the future as a hybrid approach to creating a high-quality mass-digitized corpus that also treats the source material with great care.[1]

Other MDLs provide such an important service as well. In the end, the greatest benefits will likely come to those interested in public domain works, including pre-1923 materials in the United States. In particular, nineteenth-century works are likely to see a large increase in access for several reasons, including the large amount of material that was published as well as the relative dearth of its accessibility until now. While current subjects and contemporary historical events and knowledge are well represented in the digital era, subjects from the early nineteenth and twentieth centuries may have been ignored.

Furthermore, libraries are likely to see changes in the way patrons access special collections. There should be a drop in the amount of people coming to visit archives without a specific need in mind. Instead of patrons coming just to find information on a hunch, they will be able to have greater knowledge of a collection's contents and will come seeking "other things" about the originals.

Patrons' information needs will be related less to what is found printed on the pages and more on those things that are not captured by the digital image or that are not knowable without the viewing the physical structure of the original. This might include things such as the condition of the cover; the materials from which the original was made; and the notes or marginalia that might not appear on digital scans because of light, deterioration, mold, or tight bindings.

A great example of attempting to capture the extra material often lost in other digital collections is Melville's Marginalia, a project developed at Boise State University.[2] Most digital print collections focus on allowing access to the print, and for those merely interested in the print content, the digital version would provide much-needed access. However, by creating a collection with so-called marginalia, as seen in figure 4.3, the editors of this collection provide historical information that cannot easily be replicated digitally and needs to be examined up close. In

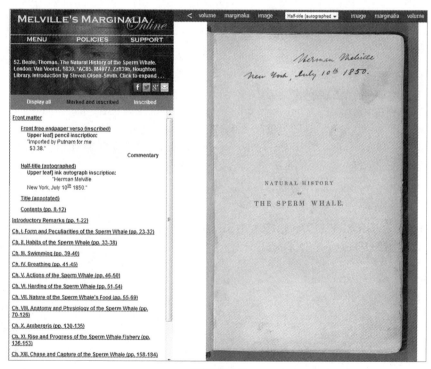

FIGURE 4.3

Image of Herman Melville's copy of Natural History of the Sperm Whale from the website Melville's Marginalia.

this way, one can perhaps see the future of MDLs. If they provide multiple versions of a text online with the various notes of readers, the result might be like a "reconstructed" commentary, similar to what one finds on SoundCloud, where users provide comments and reactions to streamed audio recordings. It may be of use to historians if all such texts containing variant readings as well as marginalia and/or personal commentary were aggregated.

STUDY SPACES

MDLs would probably have only a minor effect on student study spaces. The digital world still does not have a direct impact on the design of physical library spaces at this time. The best way that libraries can anticipate the move toward all-digital collections is through the development of smart study rooms. Current library practice appears to be moving toward such collaborative study spaces. As a result there will be a need for such spaces.

Though this is not entirely the impact of MDLs, the major shift to near-universal online content will increase pressure for spaces that meet needs while also reducing space overall in the library. The first things to go will be the stacks, especially any remaining print journals and public domain books. Next, the wide-open and undeveloped study spaces will be claimed. Eventually, all real estate within the library will need to be justified, as nearly everything besides local print and historical special collections will be transferred to digital media.

INTERLIBRARY LOAN, COURSE RESERVES, AND STUDENT TEXTBOOKS

Inter-library loan departments in libraries will be affected in positive ways by the development of MDLs. If more works are available online and in digital, full-text readable format, the need for sending books through the mail and for physical delivery systems will reduce workloads for such departments.

Course reserves would also benefit from the open content of MDLs. Faculty would be able to place works on course reserve by providing links to works in Google Books or HathiTrust, and so on. In similar ways, if full access to works were granted to member institutions of an MDL consortium, then more students would benefit from lower costs for certain works.

The new model of access derived from MDLs does not exclude publishers, who might still offer new versions of texts, either as born-digital creations or as new print materials. New editions of material will still be offered, and even as professors move to e-texts, publication opportunities still exist.

COLLECTION DEVELOPMENT: SHAPING AND WEEDING

Although Chapters 6 and 7 focus more directly on collection development, it should be mentioned that MDLs could have an effect on libraries in terms of how they shape collections. MDLs' provision of open access versions of a book will help libraries make better decisions about which books to keep or to throw away. In coordination with a consortium, libraries would be able to open up even more space for other types of uses within their traditional bricks-and-mortar structures. Remodeling the library to meet new needs and trends, such as learning commons and collaborative study rooms would be included.

Additionally, if works of major importance were somehow not part of the larger MDLs, the decision could be made by individual libraries at the local level to digitize and add the works to local institutional repositories, as well as to the major MDLs, such as Internet Archive, HathiTrust, and Google Books, as a contributor or even partner. Therefore, MDLs still have an important role to play in this aspect of librarianship. At the same time, local needs will remain of primary concern, and the decision to contribute works to MDLs will need to be weighed with local users in mind.

CONSORTIUM OPPORTUNITIES AND "STRENGTH IN NUMBERS"

Following the example of HathiTrust, it may be in many academic libraries' best interest to band together to create their own mass-digitization projects. If several large institutions with specialized collections of materials—for example, the University of Hawaii's Hawaiian and Pacific Collection—were to combine their holdings with those of other major institutions, a greater digital presence for these works would come to fruition. Although in this case the Pacific Rim Digital Library Alliance (http://prdla.org) currently fills this need somewhat, the scale is not nearly the same as it could be with an MDL. The benefits of such endeavors would be immense. Libraries would be able to function as indexers and holders of information that previous had been the realm of publishers. The benefit of a strengthened public domain and increased profiles for some more obscure or underrepresented subjects would accrue to users interested in these areas. Ultimately, the public good will only strengthen with increased availability of previously unknown or underutilized works.

PRESERVATION AND QUALITY OF DIGITAL AND PRINT ASSETS

Preservation—More Than Meets the Eye

Thus far, MDLs have taken a fairly conservative approach to the acquisition of books. They ingest collections of existing libraries that are already carefully curated, aggregate them into one massive collection, and arrange that into a singular online package. However, libraries not only acquire and house items; they also preserve them for the long term. If MDLs are to have an impact beyond access, they will have to work to ensure digital preservation as a major policy, and libraries will need to be vigilant with preservation regardless of whether they are active partners with MDLs.

It is easy for those unfamiliar with digital preservation to assume that once something is scanned into a digital format and saved on a disk or hard drive that it is therefore in a state of preservation. However, this is far from the truth. Preservation, as most libraries with digitization initiatives can attest, involves a large and varied cycle of procedures and overarching, forward-looking policies that ensure long-term sustainability. Such procedures include the following:

- Bitstream copying, which is mainly data backup
- Refreshing (i.e. copying from one medium to another), using durable or persistent media (e.g., gold CDs)
- Implementing technology preservation, which involves saving the whole technological ecosystem (e.g., CD player, Beta-Max video)
- Utilizing digital archaeology, which involves emergency saving of formats by recovering bitstreams from unreadable files
- Creating analog backups (e.g., using silver halide microfilm)
- Performing migration
- Performing replication (e.g., making multiple copies, like LOCKSS)

- Relying on standards (e.g., standard digital file formats such as JPEG, TIFF, MOV, MPEG)
- Performing normalization, which is essentially following formalized implementations procedures for various standards
- Performing canonicalization, which determines whether the essential characteristics of a document have remained intact through conversion (an issue that arises in MDLs and the conversion of print books to e-books)
- Performing emulation, which reproduces essential aspects of another computer's performance
- Performing encapsulation, the grouping of digital objects (e.g., files) with the metadata necessary for description and access[3]

Libraries currently considering the mass digitization of their collections, or joining any MDL projects such as HathiTrust or Google Books, would be wise to help create a digital preservation consortium based on the digitized works in their own right. Various options exist, including LOCKSS, MetaArchive, Glacier, and other cloud storage and digital preservation systems. LOCKSS focuses on preserving journals, but a similar approach might be used to tackle the long-term digital preservation of monographs.

Along with this procedural side, digital preservation also has a policy side. To ensure that the methods of digital preservation are followed correctly, policies need to be developed that address the needs of libraries and MDLs together. This will be important. Without them, even if the flesh is willing, so to speak, the spirit will be weak. Incentives and specific polices such as undergoing periodic audits in the vein of trusted digital repositories, or following such models as the Open Archival Information System (OAIS) will help ensure that things do not fall by the wayside or, as is often the case in for-profit endeavors, that corners are not cut for the sake of profitability.

Ultimately, for libraries and MDLs to fully work together, they will have to address funding sources and promises of long-term funding as well. Microsoft's own short-lived mass-digitization project is a sobering example of how lack of true long-term commitment and policy making can destroy the work.

Quality: Sisyphus or Hercules? Tragic or Heroic?

Quality may seem like a tangential topic, but in reality it is central to the issue of preservation in ways that may not be immediately obvious. Quality has been to date the easiest entry into the study of MDLs, especially the Google Books project. Scholars have fretted over poorly scanned pages; erroneous metadata records; and poor OCR application of texts, especially for languages that do not use the Roman alphabet.

The issue raised, therefore, becomes one of futility or utility. Is it ultimately a tragic, Sisyphean task to digitize the entire corpus of print books, or is it a Herculean, heroic task to ensure the quality of items stored within MDLs? The answer to this essential question boils down to whether it is worthwhile to spend resources to preserve poor-quality scans of books for long periods of time.

At its most basic level, we can examine how well MDLs have converted text on the pages of codicils in new digital versions. As errors occur in everything human, some texts show evidence of poor scanning, unreadable pages, or files that have become corrupted. The issue of quality in MDLs encompasses the adequacy of the scanned book to accurately reflect the information on the printed page, as well as what represents the best version of the book.

One of the workarounds for this error rate is to digitize the same book multiple times. If the same edition of *King Lear*, for example, has been scanned by ten different libraries, the odds of its accuracy and long-term quality and viability are greatly improved. Given a random distribution of errors, among ten copies it would seem likely that a complete, readable authoritative version could be created, and that authoritative version would have a greater chance of being preserved. The problem, though, that arises with attempting to ensure quality through the multiple-text digitization approach is the cost and burden of creating redundancies, as well as the costs of formulating an authoritative version.

However, there is also the issue of "low-hanging fruit." The best version of a book can change over time, but it is costly to scan multiple editions or multiple versions of the same book. In some cases, it is hard to see why Google or HathiTrust would necessarily scan another version of a book when the payoff may simply be better to scan a different title. Given the choice, it seems logical that an MDL would simply ingest an already-digitized book rather than spend the money to scan a different version of the same book.

Taking this idea to another level of abstraction, how does one rate the quality or value of items that fall outside the dominant culture? In an ideal world in which unlimited resources exist for all cultures, everything from high to low, old to new, canonized to apocryphal, would be preserved and not ranked against one another. But as the situation stands, resources remain limited, and it is not possible to preserve our cultures for the long run. Furthermore, quality becomes a cultural value, but quality as value doesn't necessarily adhere to the needs of all cultures. The dominant cultures may not see quality in certain items, and as a result, those items are inevitably passed over in favor of other things.

In this light, the prospect of safeguarding the quality of digital output can be either a tragic endeavor in which the worst of both worlds destroys the best qualities of both the print and the digital, or it can be a heroic endeavor in which the best aspects remain at the forefront and preserved for the foreseeable future.

METADATA: THE NEEDLE IN THE INFORMATION HAYSTACK

MDLs have grown out of the smaller digital collections and libraries that started in the 1990s. Yet the best of them, such as the HathiTrust and Europeana, still have to resolve issues related to the representation of monographs through simplified metadata schema. For decades the library staked its information technology reputation on the MARC record, which is perhaps one of the most detailed metadata schemes in existence, and controlled vocabularies (e.g., LCSH, MESH, AAT, TGN). The combination of these two things provided users with a high level of information accuracy but a low level of usability for patrons.

Yet the MDLs are now dealing with digital collections instead of print. In the case of the HathiTrust, this seems to be of little problem, as the project is based on the best practices of librarianship. HathiTrust's handling of multivolume works is exemplary; it bundles multiple digital files in an easy-to-find manner. However, Google Books underperforms with multivolume works. It is often too difficult, for example, to find all volumes of a multivolume work or to retrieve them in a coherent manner. This comes down to metadata. If Google did not rely entirely on the full-text search and provided better methods for describing the data itself, it might not have this problem.

It is also important to note that not all MDLs operate under standardized definitions for all the metadata they employ, and some even generate more problems in aggregate than the source collections do. For example, Google Books routinely conflates the role of author, editor, and translation in the "author" metadata fields in its online records. This is serious malpractice from a librarian's perspective, but it likely arrives from problems of crosswalking metadata sets and standards to Google's in-house standards.

For the time being, then, robust human-created and human-readable metadata remains one of the great intangible "added values" of libraries that MDLs may have a hard time replacing without more rigorous standardization. It is hard at this point to imagine that the superior metadata of libraries could be replaced by inaccurate, dumbed-down systems, yet superior technologies have sometimes been replaced by inferior ones for the sake of expediency or profit.

EXPLORATORY METHODS, EXPLORATORY SEARCHING, AND USER EXPERIENCE

This section discusses some of the basic tools librarians might use to explore and evaluate MDLs, including exploratory methods, searching, and applying both to an examination of user experience.

Exploratory Methods

Exploratory methods are used to develop a general impression of the massive digital library through more informal examinations of information. Specifically, content, scope, depth of subject matter, metadata quality, scan quality, OCR accuracy, and user experience can be explored to arrive at a more general understanding of MDLs. At this point, once the area of exploration is chosen, librarians can raise multiple questions, including the following:

- What am I looking at?
- What content is available?
- What are the functions of the software interface?
- How are the files organized?
- Are there subject headings and call numbers?
- What other metadata is available, and how accurate is it?
- Was the digital scan of the text also converted using OCR into another file format?
- Is the content accessible to patrons with disabilities?
- Is the available content relevant and useful to our patrons?

Exploratory methods can address these and many more questions. The goal is not necessarily to find a definitive quantitative answer in hard data, but to arrive at new knowledge that can be used in practical ways.

The primary benefit of exploratory methods is that they are relatively quick to implement. Examples include forecasting tools such as trend, impact and cross-impact analyses, and conventional Delphi methods. Such methods might be useful in comparing and contrasting the different MDLs. They usually do not require any expenditures. The information gained can be used to alter library policies and practices and to educate staff. The complexity of exploratory methods is generally low, and they require little preparation time or planning. For all of these reasons librarians can use exploratory methods, or these research tasks can be assigned to student assistants or paraprofessional staff.

It is, however, part of librarians' so-called tradecraft to know where the system functions well at delivering information and where its shortcomings exist. The basic point, then, of exploratory methods is to reach a basic understanding of what MDL collections have to offer and how libraries might best use them to meet a given patron's specific information needs.

Exploratory methods, however, do have a few limitations. For one, they cannot be used to answer research questions; they cannot reject, or fail to reject, null hypotheses (which is important, as science is about failure and rejection, not acceptance); they also cannot provide the data necessary for a detailed analysis of a research question. Whereas exploratory methods generate information, sometimes data is needed instead. This is where systematic methods become more important for gathering and analyzing data. However, this is outside the scope of this book.

Exploratory Searching

Unlike a traditional bricks-and-mortar library, it is not possible to wander the stacks of an MDL to gather a general sense of its collections. As a result, users and researchers must resort to other methods, such as exploratory searching. This term encompasses a wide range of activities, including keyword searching, metadata searching, subject-heading browsing, known-item searching, and general browsing.

Keyword Searching

Keyword searching (via taxonomies) can be done from a list of relevant words or from a random list of words. Creating a list of relevant words involves developing a basic taxonomy. Synonyms play a particularly important role in the process. For example, *bunny*, *rabbit*, and *Lepidorae* all refer to the same animal, but certain patron groups would prefer one term over another. A children's book is unlikely to contain the term *Lepidorae* just as a scientific monograph is unlikely to contain the term *bunny*. The development of a taxonomic list would improve the exploratory search.

The constructed list of words can also be employed as a proxy, or estimate, for the types of terms typical patrons might use. A knowledge, then, of subject-specific terms, synonyms, and patron-preferred terms would be useful to help examine the effectiveness of the MDL. Noting the terms that proved irrelevant or that yielded poor search results can help librarians understand the problems that patrons in specific user groups will have with MDLs.

As an aside, random keyword searching can also be employed in MDL analysis, but it is more useful as a systematic method. Simple approaches include random-word generation, such as by flipping through the dictionary at random points and choosing the first word that appears.

Metadata Searching

Metadata searching is the process of limiting a search to one or more metadata fields, such as title, author, publisher, publication date, and so on. There is a wide variance in the numbers and types of metadata fields used by MDLs. A specific MDL might also collect certain metadata fields for some materials but not for others. Even within a specific MDL there is variation. Some books scanned by Google Books use BISAC subject headings, Dewey decimal classification subject headings, Library of Congress subject headings, or a combination of all three.

Searching can be done by known-item searching or by selecting relevant terms. Known-item searching allows one to check holdings with a list of predetermined items. The list could be generated by a librarian's knowledge of a subject, or from bibliographies or literary canons. Searching for specific titles might help determine the appropriateness of a particular MDL for certain patron groups. It might also give insight into the coverage of rare but important materials.

Examining User Experience

Exploratory methods are well suited for helping approximate the challenges and obstacles users might confront when using an MDL. One of the best ways to explore the user interface is to conduct simple test searches. Some questions that arise at this stage include the following:

- How is the results list organized? Does it make sense?
- Is the MDL consistent in providing the same metadata fields for each book?

- Is it clear in the set results who the author is? The publisher? The publication date?
- Is it clear that the edition is the same as the one I'm looking for?
- Where do I click to access the book?
- Why can or can't I access the book?

Such questions are important to ask in order to get at patrons' specific needs when they are conducting a search. Users are often confused about the steps to take to access the information they want. The challenge for librarians and information science practitioners is to find out what users want to know and then see what problems untrained users face.

An additional issue to consider is how to serve patrons with disabilities. Certain software and hardware can be challenging for people with disabilities. Librarians are in unique positions to advocate for universal access to information. Seemingly small and insignificant features of a software program's interface can be insurmountable barriers to some. As a result, testing the interfaces for compliance with the guidelines in section 508 of the Americans with Disabilities Act (ADA) is an important aspect of examining all software, but especially MDLs, which purport to be universal tools. Librarians interested in ADA compliance might consider running the pages of MDLs and their displayed content through various web accessibility tools, including the WAVE web accessibility tool, Fangs screen reader emulator, and University of Illinois at Urbana-Champaign's Functional Accessibility Evaluator (http://fae.cita.uiuc.edu). Each of these tools provides analyses of the ADA compliance of web resources.[4] Even if this seems difficult or time consuming, librarians do have a duty to point out to those managing MDLs that a universal library also needs to be universally accessible.

65

CONCLUSION

It is clear that all librarians will have a stake in MDLs at some point. However, just because large consortia and private enterprises are running the best-known MDLs, individual librarians still have a role in vetting them for not only their bricks-and-mortar libraries and digital collections but also for their very real, flesh-and-blood patrons. Libraries will benefit from the collection development and space creating impacts of online digital books. The opportunities for creating larger alliances will surely strengthen the overall viability and accessibility of their collections.

However, the world of information science research must begin to develop strategies for examining how well they actually serve patrons. To move wholesale to the digital world will be a disservice for some patrons, even as it serves a greater number of patrons. It will be essential to develop sound methods and policies for long-term digital preservation. It will also be important for librarians to perform various exploratory methods to look at how and when the MDLs can serve users and to develop criteria for when the traditional role of the library might actually remain—as in the case of metadata—far superior to its purported replacement.

REFERENCE

Jeanneney, Jean-Noël. 2007. *Google and the Myth of Universal Knowledge: A View from Europe*. Chicago: University of Chicago Press. First published in French in 2005.

NOTES

1. Lesley Taylor, "Digitizing History: 82,000-Manuscript Collection Vatican Library Goes Online," Toronto Star, May 2, 2013, www.thestar.com/news/world/2013/05/02/digitizing_history_82000manuscript_collection_vatican_library_goes_online.html.

2. See the website Melville's Marginalia, at http://melvillesmarginalia.org; and "History of the Sperm Whale," http://melvillesmarginalia.org/tool.php?id=7&pageid=22.

3. "Digital Preservation Management," Cornell University Library, 2007, www.dpworkshop.org/dpm-eng/terminology/strategies.html.

4. See the Fangs Screen Reader Emulator (http://sourceforge.net/projects/fangs/); WebAim's Wave Web Accessibility Tool (http://wave.webaim.org/toolbar/); and University of Illinois at Urbana-Champaign's Functional Accessibility Evaluator (http://fae.cita.uiuc.edu).

Part 2

The Philosophical Issues

Chapter Five

The Copyright Conundrum—
or, How Is This Allowed?

We are the first generation to deny our own culture to ourselves.

—Tweet by James Boyle, Duke Law
School professor, @thepublicdomain

A COPYRIGHT CONUNDRUM

The story of copyright is tied inextricably to technological changes. The printing press, the development of the book itself, the adoption of cheaper materials and faster, more efficient modes of content distribution (including ocean travel, railways, automobiles, airplanes, and finally digital files and the Internet)—all these have had an impact on copyright law. The influence of these changes is not to be downplayed. In fact, copyright law in the digital age is struggling to currently keep pace with the rapid changes in digital distribution platforms, including the development of peer-to-peer sharing networks, e-book readers, digital rights management technologies and policies, and the like.

Authors are often cited as the main beneficiaries of copyright, especially in terms of marketing and piracy protection.[1] Yet most authors or creators, except for the few who actually become truly self-sufficient, rarely benefit financially from copyright protection. In fact, as scholar Paul Heald has found for most authors or creators—many of whom would likely prefer to see their work disseminated much more widely—copyright law actually creates a dampening effect on the distribution

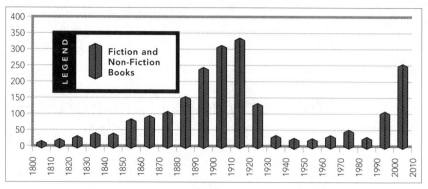

FIGURE 5.1
Copyright law severely limits accessibility to works in copyright.
The number of editions available of material from 1910 is greater
than that of the last decade. (Courtesy of Paul Heald)

70

of their works.[2] As seen in figure 5.1, although the public domain allows users to adapt and utilize content openly and without restriction for the advancement of culture, science, and society, works are being kept away from the public for much longer than ever in history. Currently, the United States is enduring a public domain freeze, and works will not begin to pass into the public domain again until 2019.[3]

So how is it possible that a series of laws set up nominally to help a particular group of people can simultaneously have a negative influence on the culture as a whole? Furthermore, how can a set of laws that are essentially antitrust in nature—creating quasi fiefdoms of cultural and intellectual matter—exist in a capitalist society, which usually encourages competition at the expense of stability?

This is the copyright conundrum, and there are reasons for this current contradictory state of affairs. These contradictions have always existed, but the appearance of MDLs has brought copyright issues to light on a much larger scale.

A BRIEF HISTORY OF COPYRIGHT

When looking at the history of copyright, both with early and recent copyright precedents, it becomes clear that the force driving the development and extension of copyright law comes not from a need to protect authors and creators—although the law does at times protect them from blatant piracy and theft—but from a need to preserve the interests of the distributors and publishers of the content. Indeed, it is often the *distributors who benefit most* from copyright laws, not authors or creators. This distinction makes many of the motives for recent copyright lawsuits that occur in the name of authors much more coherent. In *Cambridge University Press v. Becker* (see Schwartz 2012), which involved three publishers (Oxford University Press, Sage Publications, and Cambridge University Press) suing Georgia State University over copyright infringement in online course reserves, is a fine case in point (Schwartz 2012).

Copyright law has developed in tandem with technological innovations—especially the printing press and improved infrastructure—since the early 1600s, but it also began in a rather dubious manner. In England, the first copyright policies were developed as a way to curtail the free flow of information, which was seen as a destabilizing force in their society. Indeed, the first copyright office, the London Stationers' Company, was "granted a royal monopoly over all printing in England, old works as well as new, in return for keeping a strict eye on what was printed."[4] The invention of the printing press in 1440 had created a boon in the amount of texts available, but the English monarchy deemed some of those texts "seditious" and dangerous. As a result, the stationers were charged with stemming the tide of revolutionary ideas.

From this model copyright continued to develop out of this de facto monopolization of printable content. In 1709 the very first law regarding copyright was enacted, the Statute of Anne, which limited copyright length to fourteen years and

> transformed the stationers' copyright—which had been used as a device of monopoly and an instrument of censorship—into a trade-regulation concept to promote learning and to curtail the monopoly of publishers . . . . The features of the Statute of Anne that justify the epithet of trade regulation included the limited term of copyright, the availability of copyright to anyone, and the price-control provisions.[5]

Essentially, copyright shifted from a censoring role to a more regulatory one.

In the United States, the copyright laws of 1790 were written as the new nation was being developed, yet the new laws were similar to the Statute of Anne, from nearly eighty years earlier. In the United States, copyright was originally limited to one term of fourteen years, with the possibility of extension for another fourteen years.

Over the decades and into the twentieth century, however, the story of copyright is one of lengthening and increasingly stricter interpretations of the meaning of

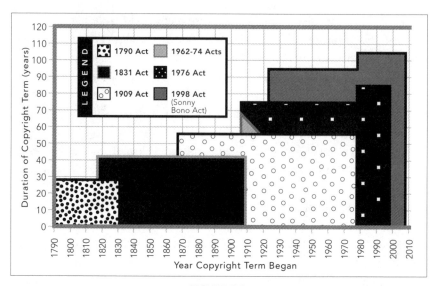

FIGURE 5.2

Copyright term lengths in the United States have increased since the original act of 1790. The current copyright length since the 1998 Copyright Extension Act is seventy years plus the life of an author.

(Chart assumes authors have created their works at age thirty-five and live for seventy years).

© Tom Bell. Creative Commons Attribution-Share Alike 3.0 Unported license.

copyright restriction. The shrinking of the public domain is a direct result of longer and more restrictive copyright protections (see figure 5.2).

Each subsequent copyright act in the United States has created longer terms for protection, and the main act that affects everyone to this day, the Copyright Act of 1976, closed several avenues for copyright lapses and granted complete protection to all works regardless of whether the creators had followed procedures to register the work or not. This carte blanche application of copyright to all works reduces confusion about whether works are copyrighted or in the public domain, but it does provide some issues in enforcement, especially with regard to orphan works.

CURRENT COPYRIGHT LAW

Overview

Despite these lengthening and increasingly strict interpretations of the rules, the basics of copyright remain the same: authors or creators (or those to whom such rights are transferred) are granted automatic rights to prevent others from making unauthorized copies or distributing their work. Without these, many argue, the livelihoods of artists, creators, publishers, and distributors of content would be in jeopardy.

The most important current statutes in US copyright law are the 1976 Copyright Act; the 1998 Copyright Term Extension Act (also known as the Sonny Bono Act, for the actor-turned-senator who initiated the law); and the 1998 Digital Millennium Copyright Act (DMCA), created partly at the behest of the largest employer in Bono's district, Disney Corporation. Each of these acts provides the pillars for current copyright law and enforcement.

The 1976 Copyright Act established some of the copyright basics currently in effect, including the granting of automatic rights without having to register the works with the Copyright Office and the increased length of protection for a work, from an earlier fifty-six-year maximum to the life of an artist plus fifty years.

The 1998 Copyright Term Extension Act increased the length of protection for a work to the life of an author plus seventy years. Given that the term was extended to meet a few specific distributors' interests, it should be expected that another extension will be in the works by the next decade. Indeed, as of summer 2013, Congress had begun to take another look at revising copyright laws and creating "the next great copyright act" at behest of the US Copyright Office (Pallante 2013).

The 1998 DMCA provided distributors much farther-reaching control over the private use and ability for users to copy digital files by criminalizing infringement. The act also proscribes people from damaging or altering any digital rights management (DRM) software or devices designed to prevent unauthorized copying. Aside from its questionable tactics of impinging upon a person's right to the private use of an item he or she has purchased, the statute has been criticized for stifling free expression and violating computer intrusion laws.[6]

Yet, despite DRM, proscriptive copyright laws, and other statutes being ostensibly more favorable to copyright holders, these limitations are not the whole story of copyright. There are several important exceptions to copyright that users of content can freely utilize.

Public Domain

The public domain is essentially any work that exists outside of copyright protection and is thus freely usable by anyone to adapt, change, or republish. However, the rationale behind creating a vital public domain is described quite well by the

Europeana Foundation, operator of the MDL of the European Union, at its website (www.publicdomaincharter.eu): "The public domain is the raw material from which we make new knowledge and create new cultural works." A commons like the public domain provides a shared basis from which new knowledge and new artistic endeavors and progress can occur. New theories, ideas, concepts, and technologies would not exist without models from previous centuries. Indeed, Isaac Newton, when describing his invention of the calculus, said, "If I have seen further it is by standing on the shoulders of giants." But with an incredibly shrinking public domain within the United States, the current length of the copyright term might be better described as giants standing on our shoulders.

Works enter the public domain for various reasons, the most common of which is age. Anything published before 1923, or unpublished before 1894, has entered the public domain. These works can be used freely by anyone without permission. Furthermore, many US states and the US government publish their works directly into the public domain, providing little or no restrictions on their use. Additionally, many works that existed before the 1976 Copyright Act have passed into the public domain through noncompliance with some of the regulations of the time. For example, if someone published a work in 1957 without affixing the © symbol to it, and failed to register that work with the US Copyright Office, then the work automatically passed into the public domain. The frequency of works passing into the public domain in this fashion is not known, but as Gerhardt (2013, 4) describes it:

> This system provided many public benefits. It fed many works into the public domain immediately, and many others entered after less than three decades. It also provided clarity, because if one knew the work was published, the presence or absence of notice clearly indicated which path was selected. When an author did not choose the path of protection, the default route led straight to the public domain.

Open Content Movements: Creative Commons, Open Access, and Open Source

The copyright laws as enforced from March 1989 have muddied the clarity that used to exist in the law. Now one must track down authors to determine the extent of permissions allowed. However, open content movements have sprouted to address this issue. There are many creators and writers who freely waive their rights using certain licenses that predetermine how users can alter, use, or even distribute their works. There is essentially a new content community growing parallel to the current copyright-restricted one. For example, the open access movement allows users to freely view, read, and comment on published materials. The other is the Creative Commons licensing movement, in which creators can predetermine the extent of the rights they wish to waive in order to allow others to use, modify, or repurpose to suit their needs by affixing a CC license to their works.

Sometimes this movement toward open content is aligned with educational or national mandates. For example, the National Institutes of Health and the National Science Foundation have mandated that data generated by public funding must be made available to all users. Other institutions have created open educational resources (OERs) to allow educators and students to enhance classroom learning objectives. One example is MERLOT, an OER content aggregator that draws content in from various repositories. Generally, current copyright law would prohibit such free exchange and reuse of content, but with specific licenses applied to works, copyright litigation can be avoided. As long as users don't abuse the license or reach beyond the tenets of fair use, then the models can work tolerably well.

Ultimately, these open access movements prove that copyright need not induce fear. The motivation for these organizations is the fostering of ideas and the exchange of information—all for the progress of disciplines.

Fair Use

Fair use is probably the strongest of all the exemptions to copyright, and it is one of the most flexible, blurred, and ultimately misunderstood of the exemptions. It is frequently referred to as breathing room to allow for the freedom of expression within copyright law.[7] Fair use has a framework of four criteria to determine whether it is permitted to use a particular copyrighted work. The four factors are the purpose and character of the use, the nature of the original material to be used, the amount and substantiality of the material used, and the economic impact that its use will have on the creator or copyright owner. The person trying to determine fair use weighs each of the four factors equally and, ideally, makes a reasoned decision on using or not using something.

If something is determined as a fair use, then the users of copyrighted materials can use the work *without written permission*. Generally, fair uses are scholarly, nonprofit, critical, and transformative in purpose. As a result, nonprofit universities and schools have a strong foundation for using works fairly, which also means that for-profit universities and businesses have a much harder time using works without permission.

Overall, fair use is widely downplayed by distributors and publishers, and even authors, to some extent. However, it is a powerful tool for providing people with the ability to comment on, change, and adapt old models and old ideas into something new. And it is a powerful exception to the seemingly authoritarian restrictions of copyright owners.

A Note on Orphan Works

Orphan works are those published materials for which it is not easy to determine the copyright owner. Sometimes companies go out of business. Sometimes children or grandchildren of the original owner are unaware that they are rightful owners of content. Sometimes authors have given up seeking compensation or claims upon their works. Sometimes people cannot be reached to secure permission. In those situations, where the copyright owner is not accounted for or is deemed unreachable, the work is determined to be an orphan work. It's still under copyright, but copyright may not be enforceable.

Yet the rights still remain firmly in the hands of the putative copyright owners. As a result, people sometimes come out of the woodwork to claim ownership. A main obstacle for MDLs with respect to copyright is the preponderance of such orphan works. The lack of express permissions to digitize and place certain works online is a huge impediment to the development of MDLs. Indeed, as of June 2013, the *Authors Guild v. HathiTrust* ruling was being contested on issues related to orphan works.[8]

The issue of orphan works is more common, though, with archives and special collections, where people's unpublished letters and accounts are afforded much longer copyright terms, and, due to the age of the documents, the copyright holders are harder to track down . The digitization of such collections often requires due diligence and good faith. As long as archives follow due diligence these precautions regarding orphan works are often unnecessary, and since letters of request to use the works are usually kept on file at an archive, most of these issues with orphan works tend not to arise.

However, the simplest solution to avoid liability has been for historical organizations to digitize their holdings but completely eschew posting the materials online.

MDLs face similar situations, but have so far, at least in the case of Google, proved much bolder in their approach.

Impact of the Digital Age

All new information technologies have had an impact on copyright law. However, the digital age has likely had the most profound of all impacts. The Internet functions both as a device that is capable of providing easy communication and as the "world's largest copy machine."[9] Thus, use of the Internet can circumvent many of the distribution and publication industries that built up around various artistic, scientific, and other cultural creations.

As a direct result of Internet users' ability to communicate and spread content verbatim, several industries, including the Recording Industry Association of America and the Motion Picture Association of America, became fearful for their livelihoods and compelled Congress to act. The Digital Millennium Copyright Act (DMCA) is one such result. By criminalizing attempts to dismantle digital rights management software or other similar technologies, the distributors of content are able to protect their livelihoods. At the same time, criminalizing the circumventing of already-questionable tactics to preserve profit margins arguably impedes the basics of fair use. In many ways, then, if people are unable to use fair use as a defense against draconian content restrictions, the future of fair use comes into question. There is some evidence, though, that courts still favor fair use despite the restrictions spelled out in the DMCA. A ruling in 2010 determined that breaking DRM software code or the restrictions imposed on the hardware for legitimate and fair use reasons should be allowed: "Merely bypassing a technological protection that restricts a user from viewing or using a work is insufficient to trigger the DMCA's anti-circumvention provision."[10] The implication may be that something considered fair use should not be cause for legal action just because the technological protections built into digital media prevent any unintended uses. For example, a person attempting to copy a CD for personal use—often considered fair use—may need to dismantle the DRM software installed into the disk to copy it. DRM software prevents a person from using the disk beyond playback, thereby encroaching on a person's potential right to repurpose and transform it, as a producer, DJ, or musician would. Suggesting the legality of dismantling overrestrictive software—if deemed a fair use, that is—would allow for the breathing room necessary for end users.

THE IMPACT OF MDLS ON COPYRIGHT LAW

It would be an understatement to say that MDLs have had some impact on copyright law. MDLs can be seen as logical extensions of the Internet's early promise of being an information superhighway. Yet there has been intense backlash from all sides against MDLs. Indeed, the two largest MDLs, HathiTrust and Google Books, have been saddled with high-profile lawsuits since the mid-to late 2000s. In this section we look at those cases and provide an overview of why they are important to libraries and the impact they are likely to have on the future of publisher-library cooperation and on both industries individually.

Authors Guild v. Google Books

Without a doubt the best-known lawsuit regarding publishers, authors, and digital libraries is *Authors Guild Inc. v. Google, Inc.*[11] At stake in this case are numerous issues, the most important of which is whether Google's digitization of millions of books can be considered fair use. The case hinges upon an analysis of Google Books and the four factors of fair use. Some commentators have argued that Google's claim of fair use may be mischaracterization of the legal framework and may eventually damage the fair use defense. Samuelson argues, for example, that "if one of Google's rivals aims to develop a commercial database like GBS [Google Book Search] when it starts scanning, it won't have a fair use leg to stand upon."[12] Additionally, Kevles (2013) finds fault with the millions of digitized magazines that are falling through the cracks and the possibility that accessibility for the blind and other disabilities is outweighed by potential reductions in civil rights.

Although Google had already begun digitizing texts in the early 2000s, the results had not been visible in its searchable online database Google Books until 2004. Initial action against Google from the Authors Guild began in 2005, less than one year after Google launched its Google Books project. By 2006, both parties had begun negotiations to settle. It wasn't until October 2008, however, that the parties proposed a settlement agreement, which included Google compensating the Authors Guild $125 million. Some of the money would be used to create the Book Rights Registry. This would allow authors or other rights holders to collect compensation from Google. The settlement was amended in 2009 and excluded foreign works published outside the United States, Canada, the United Kingdom, and Australia. The settlement was delayed further as the courts examined the settlement agreement beginning in February 2010. A ruling in March 2011 was released, rejecting the settlement.[13] As recently as May 2013, however, more plaintiffs, including the American Photographic Artists, joined the lawsuit.[14]

The amended settlement agreement was rejected on several grounds, including the fact that the agreement itself seemed to "transfer to Google certain rights in exchange for future and ongoing arrangements, including the sharing of future proceeds, and it would release Google (and others) from liability for certain future acts."[15] As the case noted, the agreement also exceeded the scope of the case itself and "would release claims well beyond those contemplated by the pleadings."[16]

In November 2013, however, the *Authors Guild v. Google* case was finally ruled on by Judge Denny Chin, who found that the fair use defense employed by Google Books with regard to its display of only "snippets" of content for copyright works was justifiable.[17] In his ruling, the judge advocated quite positively for the project:

> Google Books provides significant public benefits. It advances the progress of the arts and sciences, while maintaining respectful consideration for the rights of authors and other creative individuals, and without adversely impacting the rights of copyright holders. It has become an invaluable research tool that permits students, teachers, librarians, and others to more efficiently identify and locate books. It has given scholars the ability, for the first time, to conduct full-text searches of tens of millions of books. It preserves books, in particular out-of-print and old books that have been forgotten in the bowels of libraries, and it gives them new life. It facilitates access to books for print-disabled and remote or underserved populations. It generates new audiences and creates new sources of income for authors and publishers. Indeed, all society benefits.[18]

This ruling appears to focus primarily on the immediate social benefits that the Google Books project provides users, although the phrase "without adversely impacting the rights of copyright holders" is certainly debatable. In particular, the emphasis on "old books that have been forgotten in the bowels of libraries" is a particularly cogent point. Many of the works on Google Books are indeed out of print and their accessibility impeded by physical and organizational barriers. Additionally, publishers have chosen for various reasons, as seen in Paul Heald's research earlier in this chapter, to not republish or provide further access to them in the form of new editions.[19] Although libraries provide access to these works to those outside their main constituencies via interlibrary loan partnerships, these are costly and slower in comparison.

However, with the extremely volatile nature of for-profit business, the long-term effects of Google Books do not seem to be of as much importance in this case. It remains to be seen whether Google Books' social benefits are sustainable, especially if bottom-line profitability remains the primary mode of the project's effectiveness. Google's tendency in the past to pull the plug on various unprofitable projects should cause concern for the unpredictable future of Google Books.

Despite that it lost the case, the Authors Guild's main criticism of Google remains the same. According to the guild, Google continues to profit from its use of millions of copyright-protected books while failing to reward authors. Since the ruling the Authors Guild has stated its disagreement and dissatisfaction, and as of December 30, 2013, it had already provided a basic notice of appeal to the US Court's Second Circuit.[20] The case, therefore, is likely to continue through appeals for the foreseeable near future.

Authors Guild v. HathiTrust

Authors Guild v. HathiTrust is in some ways counterpoint to the ongoing Google Books copyright case.[21] Although there are similarities in the cases, the case against HathiTrust turns on the development of precautions and transformative uses that it appears Google never considered.

The Authors Guild contended that by digitizing and indexing several millions of works, HathiTrust committed serious copyright infringement. The HathiTrust university consortium, which includes the University of Michigan, however, defends its actions as fair use. The lawsuit began September 2011 and was ruled on October 11, 2012—in contrast to the eight-year Google Books lawsuit. In the end the judge ruled in favor of HathiTrust.

Fair use was central to the defense of HathiTrust's digitization effort. Essentially, the court held that the goal of promoting science would be met more by allowing use than by preventing it:

> The enhanced search capabilities that reveal no in-copyright material, the protection of Defendants' fragile books, and perhaps most importantly, the unprecedented ability of print-disabled individuals to have an equal opportunity to compete with the sighted peers in the ways imagined by the ADA protect the copies made by Defendants as fair use.[22]

The holding suggests that libraries that digitize materials for purposes of transformation, preservation, noncommercial use, and compliance with the Americans with Disabilities Act fall well within the fair use doctrine. Also noteworthy—and this is a flaw of the HathiTrust MDL itself—is that access to copyrighted materials is entirely limited to text mining. Actual content itself is not available for others to see. This limitation helped HathiTrust to avoid any liability in terms of copyright infringement. The court concluded: "I cannot imagine a definition of fair use that would not encompass the transformative uses made by Defendants' [mass digitization project]."[23]

The implications of this ruling are important for all libraries. As long as they stay within fair use guidelines, digitization projects of text materials have set a precedent helping to defend their actions beyond the basic preservation of materials. In this case fair use includes transformative indexing and full-text searching, preservation of source materials via digital copies, adhering to strictly noncommercial and scholarly activities, and creating collections of materials that help the visually impaired in order to adhere to the Americans with Disabilities Act.

The future may be brighter for MDLs that follow the more cautious service-oriented and educational model espoused by the HathiTrust. However, as of summer 2013 some dark clouds were gathering again. The Authors Guild filed an appeal contesting the 2012 ruling in 2013 and it remains to be seen what happens as the saga may not be over yet.[24]

Fighting for the Public Domain: Europeana

Aside from litigation, some MDLs have taken up issues within copyright and culture by attempting to change legal frameworks and take on stronger roles in advocacy. Europeana, the MDL that incorporates the cultural materials of hundreds of European cultural institutions, has created a policy for developing a stronger public domain. Europeana appears to have an active respect for and desire to encourage the development of the public domain.

Europeana's Public Domain Charter (www.publicdomaincharter.eu) states three principles for a healthy public domain. The first principle is "Copyright protection is temporary," a reminder that the statutes of copyright are meant to be short term. It can be inferred that the MDL's intent is also to suggest that the shorter the exclusivity in copyright law, the stronger the public domain will become. The second principle states, "What is in the public domain needs to remain in the public domain." Recent court cases in the United States show a trend of allowing works to be recopyrighted. For example, in *Golan v. Holder* the Supreme Court held that works can be put back into copyright protection, thus adjusting the law to allow the United States to move into better compliance with the Berne Convention for the Protection of Literary and Artistic Works, an international agreement on copyright protection first established in Berne, Switzerland, in 1886.[25] This precedent does not bode well for ensuring that works that have passed into the public domain remain there. The third principle of the Europeana Foundation is "the lawful user of a digital copy of a public domain work should be free to (re-)use, copy and modify the work." Essentially, creativity and new knowledge cannot be developed without the free use of old models, which was how cultures progressed for thousands of years.

The Europeana policy also takes other current developments in copyright to task, including the US Digital Millennium Copyright Act (DMCA) of 1998 and the Google Books project, which pairs corporate interests with cultural ones. As for the DMCA and similar decrees that criminalize what might actually be fair use, the Europeana Foundation in its Public Domain Charter avers that "no other intellectual property rights must be used to reconstitute exclusivity over Public Domain Material." The DMCA prohibits any users from dismantling data rights management software or devices in any circumstances. While this is useful for the distributors or publishers of content, it prevents users from exercising their fair use rights and could, if a work were actually in the public domain, prevent people from fully using the source material. Indeed, according to the Europeana Foundation, "No technological protection measures backed-up by statute should limit the practical value of works in the public domain."

In the case of Google Books or similar corporate-cultural hybrid projects, Europeana warns against allowing proprietary interests to lock down content by exploiting exclusive relationships. According to the Europeana Foundation, such commercial content aggregators are "attempting to exercise as much control as possible over . . . public domain works." It warns that whether in analog or in digital form, works that were freely accessible should not be compromised.

Overall, the Europeana vision is one that aligns much with many of the values of European cultural organizations as well as those of the United States—and indeed, those of the whole world. Jeanneney's cri de coeur from 2007 right after Google announced its intentions to enter the digitization game appears to have had an impact on the development of this particular MDL. Currently, though, given its size, Europeana appears to be on solid footing and poised to be a strong advocate for the free and open use of online public domain materials.

CONCLUSION

It is clear that MDLs are having a large impact on the landscape of copyright. Despite its recent victorious ruling, Google appears to have a long legal fight on its hands. Some of its problems stem from the proprietary nature of its endeavor. If Google were to abandon the primary focus on profit making or perhaps alter the fundamental purpose of their program, it might be seen in a better light. HathiTrust seems to have weathered the copyright lawsuit storm well and is poised to develop as the leader of MDLs in terms of copyright compliance and providing access to public domain works and access to those works by people with disabilities. Finally, Europeana's efforts to advocate for a strong and robust public domain make it a worthy cause to follow. Hopefully these MDLs will continue to fight for strong and clear open access of cultural content disambiguated from the profit motives of corporations.

83

REFERENCES

Gerhardt, Deborah. 2013. "Freeing Art and History from Copyright's Bondage." UNC Legal Studies Research Paper No. 2213515. http://dx.doi.org/10.2139/ssrn.2213515.

Kevles, Barbara. 2013. "Will Google Books Project End Copyright?" *AALL Spectrum* 17, no. 7 (May): 34–36, 47. www.aallnet.org/main-menu/Publications/spectrum/Archives/vol-17/No-7/google-books.pdf.

Pallante, Maria. 2013. Statement of Maria A. Pallante Register of Copyrights, US Copyright Office before the Subcommittee on Courts, Intellectual Property and the Internet Committee on the Judiciary. US House of Representatives, 113th Congress, 1st Session, March 20. www.copyright.gov/regstat/2013/regstat03202013.html#_ftn1.

Schwartz, Meredith. May 17, 2012. "Georgia State Copyright Case: What You Need to Know—and What It Means for E-Reserves." *Library Journal*, May 17. http://lj.libraryjournal.com/2012/05/copyright/georgia-state-copyright-case-what-you-need-to-know-and-what-it-means-for-e-reserves/#_.

NOTES

1. "Guild Tells Court: Reject Google's Risky, Market-Killing, Profit-Driven Project," Authors Guild, September 17, 2013, www.authorsguild.org/category/advocacy/.

2. Rebecca Rosen, "The Hole in Our Collective Memory: How Copyright Made Mid-Century Books Vanish," *Atlantic*, July 30, 2013, www.theatlantic.com/technology/archive/2013/07/the-hole-in-our-collective-memory-how-copyright-made-mid-century-books-vanish/278209/.

3. John Mark Ockerbloom, "Public Domain Day 2010: Drawing up the Lines," *Everybody's Libraries*, January 1, 2010, http://everybodyslibraries.com/2010/01/01/public-domain-day-2010-drawing-up-the-lines/.

4. "The Surprising History of Copyright and the Promise of a Post-Copyright World," http://questioncopyright.org/promise.

5. Ibid.

6. "DMCA Digital Millennium Copyright Act," Electronic Frontier Foundation, 2013, www.eff.org/issues/dmca.

7. "Guidelines and Best Practices," University of Minnesota Libraries, 2010, www.lib.umn.edu/copyright/guidelines.

8. "Authors' Orphan Works Reply: The Libraries and Google Have No Right to 'Roll the Dice with the World's Literary Property,'" Authors Guild, June 25, 2013, www.authorsguild.org/advocacy/authors-orphan-works-reply-the-libraries-and-google-have-no-right-to-roll-the-dice-with-the-worlds-literary-property/; "Remember the Orphans? Battle Lines Being Drawn in HathiTrust Appeal," Authors Guild, June 7, 2013, www.authorsguild.org/advocacy/remember-the-orphans-battle-lines-being-drawn-in-hathitrust-appeal/; see also Authors Guild v. HathiTrust, 902 F.Supp.2d 445, 104 U.S.P.Q.2d 1659, Copyr.L.Rep. ¶ 30327 (October 10, 2012).

9. Lena Groeger, "Kevin Kelly's 6 Words for the Modern Internet," *Wired Magazine*, June 22, 2011, www.wired.com/business/2011/06/kevin-kellys-internet-words/.

10. "Ruling on DMCA Could Allow Breaking DRM for Fair Use," *Electronista*, July 25, 2010, www.electronista.com/articles/10/07/25/court.says.cracking.drm.ok.if.purpose.is.legal/#ixzz2do0ASJv5.

11. Authors Guild v. Google, Case 1:05-cv-08136-DC, Document 1088 (November 14, 2013).

12. Pamela Samuelson, "Google Books Is Not a Library," *Huffington Post*, October 13, 2009, www.huffingtonpost.com/pamela-samuelson/google-books-is-not-a-lib_b_317518.html.

13. Andrew Albanese, "Publishers Settle Google Books Lawsuit," *Publisher's Weekly*, October 5, 2012, www.publishersweekly.com/pw/by-topic/digital/copyright/article/54247-publishers-settle-google-books-lawsuit.html.

14. Mike Masnick, "American Photographic Artists Join the Lawsuit against Google Books," *Techdirt*, April 25, 2013, www.techdirt.com/articles/20130416/17225622732/american-photographic-artists-join-lawsuit-against-google-books.shtml.

15. Andrew Albanese and Jim Milliot, "Google Settlement Is Rejected," *Publisher's Weekly*, March 22, 2011, www.publishersweekly.com/pw/by-topic/digital/content-and-e-books/article/46571-google-settlement-is-rejected.html.

16. Ibid.

17. Stephen Shankland, "Judge Dismisses Authors' Case against Google Books," *CNET News*, November 14, 2013, http://news.cnet.com/8301-1023_3-57612336-93/ judge-dismisses-authors-case-against-google-books/.

18. "Judge Denny Chin Google Books Opinion," *CNET News*. 2013, www.scribd.com/ doc/184176014/Judge-Denny-Chin-Google-Books-opinion-2013-11-14-pdf.

19. Rebecca Rosen, "The Hole in Our Collective Memory: How Copyright Made Mid-Century Books Vanish," *Atlantic*, July 30, 2013, www.theatlantic.com/technology/ archive/2013/07/the-hole-in-our-collective-memory-how-copyright-made-mid -century-books-vanish/278209/.

20. "Authors Guild Appeals Google Decision," *Publishers Weekly*, December 30, 2013, www.publishersweekly.com/pw/by-topic/digital/content-and-e-books/article/60492 -authors-guild-appeals-google-decision.html.

21. Authors Guild v. HathiTrust, 902 F.Supp.2d 445, 104 U.S.P.Q.2d 1659, Copyr.L.Rep. ¶ 30327 (October 10, 2012).

22. Quoted in the American Council on Education's Amicus Brief: *Authors Guild v. HathiTrust Digital Library*, June 4, 2013, www.acenet.edu/news-room/Pages/ Amicus-Brief-Authors-Guild-v-HathiTrust-Digital-Library.aspx.

23. Ibid.

24. "Remember the Orphans? Battle Lines Being Drawn in HathiTrust Appeal," Authors Guild, June 7, 2013, www.authorsguild.org/advocacy/remember-the-orphans-battle -lines-being-drawn-in-hathitrust-appeal/.

25. Golan v. Holder. 132 S. Ct. 873 (2012).

Chapter Six

Collection Development— or, How Did I Get This?

This chapter examines the issues related to collection development. Often the discussion around collection development appears to be limited to binaries. Either one can afford to purchase everything like Harvard University and other similarly well-endowed institutions can, or one cannot. Generally, since one cannot, something gives way—even Harvard recently described current database subscription costs as "fiscally unsustainable."[1]

In the face of reduced funding, all libraries, whether they are public or private, academic or special, have needed to stretch their budgets. As a result, all libraries at some point in their organizational life cycles have had to develop sound methods and policies to be more selective to remain open; this will even include Google Books, if Google chooses to keep it around.

In discussing collection development and collection diversity, one must be reminded that these are interrelated. Collection development cannot proceed without a fully realized plan. At the same time, collection development, much like the canonization of texts within specific disciplines, hinges as much upon what one leaves out of a collection as on what one chooses to add.

The development of collections, then, cannot reasonably occur without some discerning methodologies, which might affect how well one can represent diverse points of view within a collection. Add financial feasibility to the issue, and one is left with dwindling capabilities to gather all possible materials, even as institutions are awash in information.

Ryan James contributed to this chapter.

COLLECTION DEVELOPMENT

While some massive digital libraries (MDLs) have attempted to create fully accessible digital collections based on sound collection development polices, it remains to be seen whether a successful comprehensive MDL can solve the needs of their numerous and often undefined end users.

Libraries spend numerous hours honing, refining, and shaping their collections to meet the anticipated needs of their users. For the most part, libraries are going to have, if not a well-defined collection development policy, at least a well-defined set of users and a specific community they have been chartered or charged to serve. According to the Texas State Library and Archives Commission, for example, "over 77 percent of elementary school libraries, 93 percent of middle/junior high school libraries, and 74 percent of high school libraries have a collection development policy."[2] Although the focus of the report is K–12 libraries in Texas, academic, public, and special libraries nationally collectively make use of collection development policies at similar rates. It is the rare library that does not employ a policy of some sort, even if it is a bare-bones outline.

This obvious need for policy development therefore reflects the ongoing importance of guidance and principles for selecting materials that end users want. Libraries' collection policies usually outline who their communities are and how the library will meet community members' needs. As a guiding document, the collection development policy shapes and creates the physical and virtual collection in the image of its constituent parts and stakeholders. Of course, it is a difficult process to anticipate user needs while also remaining true to core institutional values, so the policy document helps shape and balance those occasionally opposing sides. Without the guidance, so-called mission creep, which is essentially the loss of organizational focus, can enter into even the best managed libraries.

The need for a collection development policy also reflects the ongoing need for justification of expenditures in the face of changes in levels in funding. As state budgets have lately tended to contract during the economic downturn and then fail to rebound to pre-downturn levels, such policies provide official justification for money spent on content. As content in databases also becomes more bundled and more difficult to differentiate, the need also increases for policies to back up hard decisions about dropping extremely expensive "package deals" with database vendors.

The same principles are true for MDLs. Each of the massive digital libraries discussed in this book—with the sole exception of Google Books, which has stated a desire to digitize everything—rely on base collections that have at their hearts specific collection development policies. The following will look at some of the practices and implications of collection development in the HathiTrust, Europeana, Library of Congress's American Memory, and the Open Content Alliance.

HathiTrust: Collection Development as a Tool for Aggregation

The HathiTrust's collections are developed in coordination with its consortium and institutional partners. What is added to the HathiTrust MDL must also follow specific guidelines related to digitization, copyright, and public domain status. The works added to HathiTrust are subject to the following guidelines:

> Examples of collection development activities that might be pursued include:
>
> 1. developing particular types of collections within the HT corpus, such as comprehensive or distinctive collections in particular areas that build on participant strengths
> 2. exploring opportunities for digitization and collaboration with other initiatives
> 3. developing a shared approach to government documents that capitalizes on the work undertaken by CIC [Committee on Institutional Cooperation]
> 4. attempting to attract and aggregate additional public domain content
> 5. leveraging the HathiTrust corpus to manage print collections both amongst and beyond the HT partner libraries, including extramural partnerships with third party organizations.[3]

It is interesting to note that the HathiTrust is concerned with aggregating content that exists beyond the physical boundaries of its multiple consortia and institutions—as is Google Books. It recognizes, quite rightly too, that it does not encompass all content—despite its numerous partners and immense sizes. Because it understands this limitation, HathiTrust can therefore focus its energy on quality content development.

Significantly, the HathiTrust is also explicit in its desire to improve upon and gather together materials in the public domain. Admittedly, not everything found within the public domain has been identified as such and has been digitized, and some works that are considered in the public domain may actually be copyrighted. The incompleteness of the Internet Archive, for example, is a good indicator of this.

The attempt to make public domain acquisitions a significant pillar of the collection development policy works in the HathiTrust's favor from a copyright perspective. The Copyright Review Management System, developed at the University of Michigan with National Leadership Grant support from Institute for Museum and Library Studies, helps fulfill the promise of the HathiTrust's collection development policies and provides evidence of the HathiTrust's good-faith efforts in ensuring that copyrighted works remain protected but not at the expense of the public domain.[4]

However, some inherent limitations of the HathiTrust's collections become magnified as a result of the contents found in its partnering libraries, especially those that focus primarily on English-language academic collections. Issues of diversity in the available content come to the fore. Chapter 7 examines this issue in greater detail. However, it is important to note at this point that distortions and gaps in the aggregated collection could be diminished if the HathiTrust were to recruit institutions that held collections for historically underrepresented groups such as Latinos. Despite this, however, the HathiTrust's development of collections appears to be built on a very solid foundation.

Google Books: The Extreme Case of Aggregated Assault

Google Books' policy for developing its MDL appears to be very simple: *digitize everything*. In the history of libraries, such ambition is not unheard of. The famed ancient library of Alexandria, the Library of Congress, and any national library looking to collect everything published related to a particular country are notable examples of such omnivorous, wide-reaching ambition. Yet these are time-consuming and costly efforts that require extreme amounts of funding and personnel. In the case of Google Books, the ambition is even greater: to digitize and gather *everything in the world*. This is not an overstatement. Google is on the record stating that it wants to digitize all of the estimated 129,864,880 books in existence.[5]

This practice of mass digitization and mass aggregation eliminates the inconvenience of having to develop a solid collection development policy. If one wants to digitize everything, then one's collection policy is to gather everything. But this is as ambitious in scope as it is unrealistic. It is possible that Google Books might never achieve this, as new books are published in print form yearly—and not all are available with digital counterparts. Some works made with high-quality materials, nonstandard or handcrafted paper, or three-dimensional forms are preferable to many readers as solid objects and not as digital facsimiles.

Furthermore, the estimation of 129 million books in existence in the world may be flawed. It is not accurate to rely on ISBN numbers as Google does to help index and estimate its book holdings, as many countries, including Japan, did not adopt ISBNs until the 1960s or 1970s. The differentiation between serials, multivolume works, multiple editions, and even the concept of books is unclear as well. Does Google consider the fifty-one volumes of the Harvard Classics as one book, with one record, as in a library catalog or the HathiTrust, or are they fifty-one separate books? Does the second edition of volume 13 of the Harvard Classics really warrant digitization if the first edition is available? A "digitize everything" approach does not suitably answer such questions.

Endeavoring to digitize all books is not so much a collection development policy as it is an avoidance of one on a massive scale. To choose to digitize everything is to perform the same thing in terms of digital collections as to perform a keyword search for which the set results are like that of the Google Search: a mixture of high and low culture with only relevance ranking, which can be manipulated by both black-hat and white-hat search engine optimization, to determine whether it is a satisfactory result.

At the same time, endeavoring to digitize all content will also include books of a questionable nature, including the literatures of hate, pornography, and other provocative or even dangerous materials. Yet despite Google Books' intention to digitize everything, given Google's secrecy, it is unclear whether it has digitized materials that are considered hate speech, libelous, or offensive to various groups.

The digitize everything approach only means that some books will be missed—especially those not held by Google's partners—but also it means that a lot of unnecessary or spurious or poorly written materials may be added to the collection, further diluting the efficacy of collecting something in the first place.

Taking this a step further, in the case of dangerous or controversial materials, patron privacy becomes an issue as well. Traditional libraries have a tradition of safeguarding patron information as much as possible. Google sells patron information. Google has also recently been identified as one of the companies cooperating with the National Security Agency in spying on American citizens.[6] Google has also conducted surveillance of its own.[7] This invasion of privacy is completely at odds with the "do no evil" sloganeering that the company likes to espouse, and it is anathema to the foundation of libraries—including online digital libraries, massive or otherwise—as safe havens for research.

It's important to note that I'm not singling out Google in these criticisms. All massive digital libraries face issues of content appropriateness, sustainability, and patron privacy. The problem is that Google has yet to fully articulate responses to these issues and its lack of a realistic collection development policy as well as its lack of transparency does not alleviate misgivings.

Other MDLs: Collection Development and the Public Domain

The Internet Archive, the Library of Congress's American Memory project, and Europeana each has clear policies for the development of collections. All have strongly pursued digitizing and providing access to materials in the public domain. As a result, the public domain has a direct impact on the development of viable MDLs.

Europeana, as described in chapter 5, has a strong mission to protect the public domain and to allow access to and preserve use of such materials for all people. Its philosophy is clear: the stronger the public domain, the stronger the digital library.

The Internet Archive explicitly states as its content policy: "You may contribute content to the Internet Archive if it's in the public domain or if you own the rights to it."[8] Its collection development policy is a bit more complicated in that it also includes multimedia—audio, video, and the like—as well as web content. Its Wayback Machine crawls the Web and indiscriminately copies material unless ordered not to. This comprehensive approach is similar to Google Books in that all web content is ultimately the goal of the Internet Archive. However, where Internet Archive differs from Google Books is in its much stronger respect for and compliance with copyright laws.

The Library of Congress also advocates for a strong public domain. Its American Memory project focuses primarily on those materials of historic American interest. As a government organization, the Library of Congress also has a public mandate to provide open access and public domain materials published by the federal government.

The Open Content Alliance's Open Library also provides access to many books that have been converted into the DAISY format (**D**igital **A**ccessible **I**nformation **S**ystem), which is a set of digital files that allows for greater accessibility (i.e., provides digital audio and text markup versions). The HathiTrust lawsuit result in which materials converted to formats compliant with the Americans with

Disabilities Act were determined to be fair use also hammers home this point. The public domain and collection development go hand in hand with MDLs.

CONCLUSION

It is clear that MDLs will benefit from collection development policies. HathiTrust's collection development policy clearly delineates a vision for the digital corpus that follows library and information science principles. Especially promising with its policy is the awareness of a need to expand its range of partnerships and to increase its public domain holdings.

Google Books, in contrast, does not seem to have a policy aside from digitize everything. While this attempt at comprehensiveness is audacious, it also results in an incoherent policy that depends on circumstance, chance, and the willingness of partnering institutions and libraries as well as individuals. It is hoped that coherence will arise the greater the Google Books corpus becomes, but that does not seem likely at this point. Issues of collection comprehensiveness and above all privacy become paramount the larger the corpus becomes.

Finally, the policies of such institutions as the Internet Archive, Europeana, Open Content Alliance, and the Library of Congress show that by focusing on the needs of specific users or specific content, greater depth and user satisfaction can be reached. The Open Content Alliance's attempt at providing access to DAISY-readable books is a good example of this. Europeana, the Internet Archive, and American Memory focus on public domain works, which allows them to provide a better service as well. If they choose not to bother with copyrighted works, they will likely avoid the legal entanglements currently bogging down Google Books and, to a lesser extent, the HathiTrust.

In the end, guiding principles outlined in collection development policies still provide the best way for the managers and directors of MDLs to balance user needs and organizational principles.

NOTES

1. Ian Sample, "Harvard University Says It Can't Afford Journal Publishers' Prices," *Guardian*, April 24, 2012, www.theguardian.com/science/2012/apr/24/harvard -university-journal-publishers-prices.

2. Ester Smith, "Library Collection," 2011, Texas State Library and Archives Commission, www.tsl.state.tx.us/ld/pubs/schlibsurvey/chIIIsec4.html.

3. "Collections Committee Charge," www.hathitrust.org/wg_collections_charge.

4. "IMLS National Leadership Grant-CRMS World," University of Michigan Library, 2013, www.lib.umich.edu/imls-national-leadership-grant-crms-world.

5. Joab Jackson, "Google: 129 Million Different Books Have Been Published," *PC World*, August 6, 2010, www.pcworld.com/article/202803/google_129_million_different _books_have_been_published.html.

6. Barton Gellman and Ashkan Soltani, "NSA Collects Millions of E-Mail Address Books Globally," *Washington Post*, October 14, 2013, www.washingtonpost.com/world/ national-security/nsa-collects-millions-of-e-mail-address-books-globally/2013/10/14/ 8e58b5be-34f9-11e3-80c6-7e6dd8d22d8f_story.html.

7. Nathan Newman, "Why Google's Spying on User Data Is Worse Than the NSA's," *Huffington Post*, July 1, 2013, www.huffingtonpost.com/nathan-newman/why-googles -spying-on-use_b_3530296.html.

8. "Frequently Asked Questions," Internet Archive, https://archive.org/about/faqs.php.

Chapter Seven

Collection Diversity—or, Why Is This Missing?

DIVERSITY OF CONTENT: WHY IS THIS MISSING?

The American Library Association (ALA) actively promotes diversity in collections and urges libraries to "collect materials not just representative of dominant societal viewpoints, but also of the views of historically underrepresented groups within society" (LaFond 2000). This stance encourages libraries to broaden collections so that people might be challenged as well as inspired. The root of academic freedom, central to the ALA's core mission, lies with this need for collection diversity. Without it, libraries would be merely mirrors of dominant cultures rather than spectra holding an array of cultures.

However, given the current limitations on budgets facing all libraries, as well as the sheer numbers of materials published yearly, complete diversity cannot exist in any library, even the best-funded ones. However, that does not mean that libraries cannot at the very least attempt to meet the needs of multiple users.

Diversity is directly related to a library's collections development policy. For example, the University of Hawaii at Manoa is one of the world's largest collectors of Hawaii- and Pacific-related materials, focusing as much on the Japanese and Okinawan immigrant experience as on the native Hawaiian experience. Its collection development policy fuels its commitment to diversity, and vice versa. Yet its mission is one that must remain focused purely on its constituents. It is entirely unreasonable, for example, to expect a small, private, liberal arts institution like Kenyon College in Gambier, Ohio, for example, to collect Hawaiian and Pacific materials to such a large degree. No one would accuse the college's library of not being diverse enough just on the basis of the number of Hawaiian and Pacific materials in its collection. Some context and intention needs to be factored in.

Nevertheless, diversity is an important aspect of developing collections. Without a strong sense of constituents, one's collections may not adequately address user needs. MDLs are no different. The diversity of content may not be ideal in MDLs. Indeed, there are specific issues related to diversity of content within MDLs, including Google Books, HathiTrust, Internet Archive, and Open Content Alliance (Weiss and James 2013). But given the ability of MDLs to quickly create collections, the issues involved may be easier to solve than those of bricks-and-mortar institutions.

How MDLs Were Created Leads to Concerns about a Lack of Diversity

The diversity of content in the Google Books project or any of the other MDLs remains at the mercy of the partnerships the MDL has created. In the case of Google Books the partners added include collections from Spain, Germany, and France, as well as a major Japanese collection. Given the huge number of books and languages in the world, one must question whether such partnerships are actually fruitful. To have universal coverage, one would need to add everything. However, as discussed in chapter 6, given the physical limitations of books, this is not a feasible outcome for creating a digital corpus of everything printed. Of course, it is also important that at least MDLs find partners to fill in the missing subject matters. In this case, something is better than nothing.

For the HathiTrust, the same issues exist. The number of partners is large, but still not worldwide comprehensive. According to its online statistics, the percentage of English-language books in the MDL remains at about 50 percent. Of the top ten languages represented, 60 percent are Indo-European, with one, Latin, a dead language. Two are East Asian languages (Chinese and Japanese) and one is Slavic (Russian).[1] By world population and the number of cultural artifacts created by various cultures—especially those that are older than the United States by millennia—the collections are disproportionately skewed toward the English language. Again, like the Google Books project—and in part because many of the HathiTrust partners are shared with Google Books—the issue of the source materials calls into question the ability of MDLs to create truly diverse collections. Figure 7.1 shows the distribution of languages. English dominates. For every English title there is one in a different language.

For works in the public domain, this proportion skews even further to English— about 60 percent of titles in the public domain are English. Perhaps this reflects the

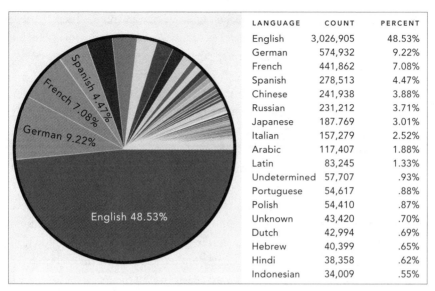

LANGUAGE	COUNT	PERCENT
English	3,026,905	48.53%
German	574,932	9.22%
French	441,862	7.08%
Spanish	278,513	4.47%
Chinese	241,938	3.88%
Russian	231,212	3.71%
Japanese	187.769	3.01%
Italian	157,279	2.52%
Arabic	117,407	1.88%
Latin	83,245	1.33%
Undetermined	57,707	.93%
Portuguese	54,617	.88%
Polish	54,410	.87%
Unknown	43,420	.70%
Dutch	42,994	.69%
Hebrew	40,399	.65%
Hindi	38,358	.62%
Indonesian	34,009	.55%

FIGURE 7.1
HathiTrust data visualization showing the
top ten languages represented in their collections.

needs of the faculty and students at the academic institutions currently partnering with the HathiTrust. It is quite telling that the second- and third-largest collections of works are German and French, while Spanish, the second most-spoken language in the United States, trails at a distant fourth. Only 4.48 percent of the HathiTrust online collection is in Spanish, yet 36 million people (roughly 12 percent of the population) in the United States speak Spanish as their primary language. In contrast, only about 1.3 million (or .41 percent) speak French and only about 1.1 million (about .35 percent) speak German, yet the HathiTrust collections include 7 percent and 9.2 percent of those languages respectively.[2] What accounts for this lack of alignment in terms of population and language representation? Why would German, for example, despite the small percentage of people actually speaking it in the home anymore, be more prevalent in the HathiTrust collections? These questions are examined more closely in the next section.

MDLs' Coverage of Traditionally Underrepresented Groups in the United States

Weiss and James (2013) focused their first study on the rate of metadata errors found in Google Books. They found a roughly 36 percent rate of error and followed this up with an investigation of the diversity of English-language content, in particular in terms of books on or originating from Hawaii and the Pacific. There were significant gaps found in the coverage, in particular a number of scannable books in the public domain did not appear in the Google Books corpus (Weiss and James 2013).

During the peer-review process for their 2012 study, however, the authors were asked why they hadn't compared the results with the HathiTrust, Internet Archive, or other similar mass book-digitization project. In their follow-up study of Spanish-language book coverage, they took other MDLs into account and compared the results of language coverage. The results of the study were also intriguing and helped to point out further gaps in the diversity of content (Weiss and James 2013).

As figure 7.2 reveals, Google Books generally did not show large differences in the coverage of Spanish-language and English-language books from a random sample of eight hundred books (four hundred in Spanish, and four hundred in English) that were also in the library catalog at California State University, Northridge. In comparison, HathiTrust showed fewer overall Spanish-language titles than Google Books (nearly twice as many had no record and were therefore not in the HathiTrust's collection). Both MDLs had similar amounts of books that were

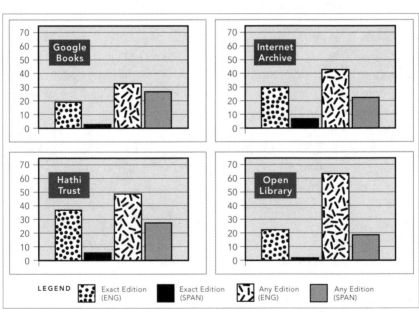

FIGURE 7.2

Levels of coverage of Spanish versus English books available as fully accessible texts (full view) in four MDLs.

(Andrew Weiss)

available in full view, however. This suggests that the two MDLs have determined the same titles to be in the public domain. It may be that many of the same titles were digitized by one or the other and then shared. But looking again at the number of Spanish-language books with no record in the HathiTrust, it seems that they have not been digitized because their partners do not have the books.

Considering, however, the percentage of Spanish-language books in the HathiTrust system and the lack of coverage found in the Weiss and James (2013) study, it becomes clear that attempting to create a universal library without taking the potential audience into account will only serve to accentuate the holes in a collection. The sample taken from California State University, Northridge—a federally designated Hispanic-serving institution—draws out these contrasts. If HathiTrust's partnering institutions do not have a priority for certain subjects or languages (e.g., Spanish-language books), then the collection will reflect those gaps. This is clear. Despite Hispanics being the largest minority in the United States (with a population of 55 million) and Spanish being spoken at home by 12 percent of US households, the HathiTrust's collection contains only a small percentage of Spanish-language books.

Again, this is a reflection of the priorities of HathiTrust's partners. The lack of representative diversity becomes obvious when one looks at current population demographics and the amount of Spanish-language books in their collection. If libraries and universities exist to serve their students, then some shifts in focus of not only subject matter offered in curriculum but also types of materials offered (e.g., Spanish-language versions of texts) will have to occur.

University libraries have historically tended not to collect scholarly and academic titles in the Spanish language. French, German, and Latin (and ancient Greek) are much more traditionally identified as the languages used in certain disciplines in academia, especially history, philosophy, religious studies, medicine, and physics. Let us not forget that the current university system grew out of the German model and that scholarship itself was dominated by that language until very recently. Perhaps this perception of Spanish as secondary in the academic world will change over time as more Spanish speakers and Hispanics attend college in the United States. Furthermore, the percentages of French, German, and Latin books currently found in university library collections will likely fade as demographics and political fortunes shift. It appears that HathiTrust's collections, out of no fault of its own, lag behind the real world by a generation or two. The collection likely best represents the emphasis of the various digitization partners as they would appear in the latter half of the twentieth century.

Libraries are slow to change or weed their collections, and it is possible that the underrepresentation of Spanish is a symptom of mass-digitization projects in general: they are relying on collections of materials that may be outdated to begin with. Digitization becomes a snapshot of a period of time (the mid- to late 2000s) for specific academic libraries and reflects the priorities of the institutions at that time.

Future Directions

It is clear that there is much to be read in the changes of a library collection's makeup. It is hoped that those studying MDLs in the future would be able to access snapshots of the digital library collection at various points in time. This will help researchers and historians to track numerous changes not only in libraries but also in departments, in college and university policies, and in the overall changing demographics of college students in the United States.

The studies conducted by James and Weiss have focused on just a few of the historically underrepresented groups in the United States. There are other possible directions to take as well. A future study of mine will involve a look at Japanese-language coverage and collections in MDLs. Comparisons between Hawaiian and Pacific, Spanish-language, and Japanese-language collections (each of which is considered a traditionally underrepresented group in the United States) would be fruitful to assess the levels of diversity found in such "universal" digital libraries. Further studies might also look at how aboriginal and Native American texts might be represented in such MDLs. In the case of Japan, for example, one might consider examining the representation of Zainichi Koreans, Ainu, or Okinawan cultures, all underrepresented groups in Japan, in MDLs.

European Criticism and
Approaches to Content Diversity

Jeanneney's critique of Google in his 2007 book has been referenced often in this book and in many other places. It remains a singularly important critique of not only Google's worldview but also its methods, which result in the possible marginalization of not only cultural institutions but whole industries and societal classes as well.

It appears that many European institutions have taken Jeanneney's advice seriously. Gallica, Europeana, and other institutions have attempted to take very "non-Google" approaches to their MDLs. Gallica is a digital cultural portal for the

French language. As such, it remains an important counterpoint to American or Anglo-centric projects. Even the HathiTrust has trouble being convincing about having acceptable levels of diversity in its collections. For example, only 7 percent of its collection actually contains French-language materials. It is unclear what the breakdown for Google Books actually is. Attempts to find this information and attempts to contact Google Books staff were not answered. Nevertheless, it is quite likely that Google Books' level of diversity is similar to that of other non-English languages, especially as its range of partners is just as limited as, say, the HathiTrust's. Essentially, this brings us back to the first part of our discussion: a massive digital collection development policy of digitizing everything.

To combat ethnocentric and language-centric collection development, it appears that many of the European models have attempted to gather works in the languages of their country. It may be that each language would need to develop its own MDL to ensure that the fruits of a culture are not marginalized. In the case of Google, its overreach is a matter of stepping on so many cultural, institutional, and economic boundaries. Yet the goals remain the same: to digitize everything that can be digitized. That driving force is creating ever-larger digital libraries, though it is possible that things will fall through the cracks.

POSITIVE TRENDS IN MDLS' DIVERSITY

However, not all is wrong in the world of MDLs. In fact, the aggregation of so much content online under a single search interface is itself a revolutionary undertaking. These are clearly the days of miracles and wonder. Some positive impacts on the aggregation of much content are clear. For example, a study by Chen in 2012 regarding OCLC records explains that, under the conditions of their study, any book in the Google Books project is mappable to the OCLC world catalog. Furthermore as of April 2013, OCLC announced it would be adding Google Books and HathiTrust records into its WorldCat system, creating an ever-larger system for finding books.

Second, the HathiTrust's collections—though obviously dominated by English—nonetheless provide access to more than 420 languages. This diversity shows that the long tail of online consumerism can also be satisfied by nonprofit, educational endeavors. If more public domain works in languages with fewer speakers than English are able to make it online, there is hope that those languages might be saved or preserved. In many ways, the HathiTrust, or any MDL for that matter, can provide the digital backbone to preserve the cultures and languages of marginalized or endangered communities.

Third, many libraries are starting to link their collections to Google Books or HathiTrust through their own online catalogs. This can provide a better way to track and target the books they need to improve their own diversity in holdings. If all the public domain full-access books were cataloged and linked outward to the source materials, or if the source materials were downloaded and added to a local library's collection, a greater number of people would be able to access this material as well. Perhaps using these open access, public domain materials will help spur a renaissance in multicultural, multilanguage, extremely diverse collection building. This will also allow other libraries to focus their limited and sometimes shrinking budgets on those books that they definitely need. These libraries can target new materials or other materials that they might never have considered before, especially if usage statistics are employed to keep track of the materials.

CONCLUSION

In the end collection development and collection diversity are two sides of the same coin. One needs a development policy to avoid the pitfalls of catering only to the dominant culture. The omnivorous approach of Google Books could be applied on a smaller scale to involve singular languages or cultures. However, in the case of the HathiTrust, the collections digitized represent a lag in time. What we are looking at—4.5 percent Spanish-language books—is a historical collection development policy time lag. The choice to focus on English, German, and French likely goes back 150 years to the very beginnings of higher education in the United States. Libraries had to prioritize on the basis of their users' needs, which in the nineteenth century focused on the main languages of scholarly communication: French and German. Those needs have obviously changed in the light of not only alterations to the way the university itself communicates, the subjects offered, the ascendance of the English language in international communication, and the Hispanic immigration and the number of Spanish speakers in the United States. Finally, although there are gaps in coverage, the technology driving MDLs that allows one to better see those gaps and fill them has never been better.

REFERENCES

Chen, Xiaotian. 2012. "Google Books Assessments: Comparing Google Books Content with WorldCat Content." *Online Information Review* 36, no. 4: 507–16. doi: 10.1108/14684521211254031

Jeanneney, Jean-Noël. 2007. *Google and the Myth of Universal Knowledge: A View from Europe.* Chicago: University of Chicago Press. First published in French in 2005.

LaFond, Deborah M., Mary K. Van Ullen, and Richard D. Irving. 2000. "Diversity in Collection Development: Comparing Access Strategies to Alternative Press Periodicals." *College and Research Libraries* 61, no. 2: 136–44.

Weiss, Andrew, and Ryan James. 2013. "An Examination of Massive Digital Libraries' Coverage of Spanish Language Materials: Issues of Multi-Lingual Accessibility in a Decentralized, Mass-Digitized World." Presentation at the International Conference on Culture and Computing, Ritsumeikan University, Kyoto, Japan, September 16.

NOTES

1. "HathiTrust Languages," www.hathitrust.org/visualizations_languages.
2. "Language Use," US Census Bureau, 2011, www.census.gov/hhes/socdemo/language/.

Chapter Eight

Access—or, Why Can't I Get This?

There is no question that we are in a time of great flux in the publishing world. The well-established and mutually beneficial relationships between publishers and libraries have changed. Some of these relationships are reaching their breaking points as journal and online database prices increase, and the licensing of e-book content threatens to render irrelevant copyright law's exhaust rule, which allows purchasers of copyrighted materials to dispose of them as they see fit (lend, resell, or discard). Access has the potential to become universal, but barriers—for better or for worse—still exist that prevent 100 percent fully open and sharable content. In examining open access the discussion shifts from one about online open access journals to the more specific needs of e-books and monographs. This chapter explores the issues of content access in MDLs and some of the finer points of open access, including the gold, green, and platinum open access models.

THE OPEN ACCESS PHILOSOPHY
AND HOW IT APPLIES TO MDLS

Ask any librarian how he or she feels about databases and you're likely to get a mixed answer. An unbelievable amount of content is available for users, they'll say, but the costs of journals have skyrocketed into the tens of thousands of dollars per title. The economic drain is palpable and unsustainable. Harvard University

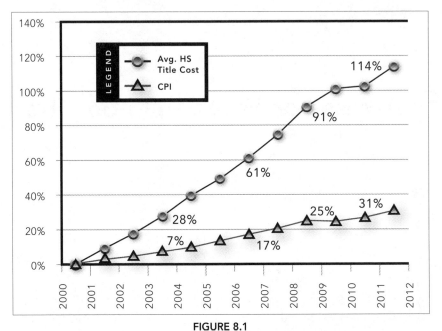

FIGURE 8.1

Costs of journals by discipline in comparison to Consumer Price Index.

(Courtesy of University of California San Francisco Library)

Library, one of the premier research libraries in the United States, if not the world, recently stated that the situation was unsustainable, even for its impressive budget.[1]

What has caused this situation? On the one hand, the publishers appear to be practicing ruinous price gouging by greatly outpacing the Consumer Price Index during the decade of the 2000s (see figure 8.1). Libraries expend far greater amounts of money on online journals than ever before, and prices continue to rise. Yet more people have more access to more information than ever before. In fact, when looking at the number of downloads per user or downloads per article versus overall costs, the cost-per-use ratios may not be so ruinous, especially if the ratios translate to a few dollars per article. Libraries may sometime be getting their money's worth, even if that initial sticker shock can be hard to handle.[2] What is missing in figure 8.1 is how many users have accessed these materials—it's likely that the number of users has grown along with the price.

Yet some of the issues raised earlier in this book regarding the destruction of the middle class via the advent of the Internet and some of its impact on destabilizing established markets are also at play here. There is a real chance that many small to midsize publishers, especially university presses, will be driven out of business because of the open distribution and piracy of published content. Larger publishers are also seeing a drop in profits, even though they still turn profits.

One current solution to the issue has been to implement open access as a policy for libraries, publishers, and universities. There are two main types of open access: gold and green. These types of open access, while linked by commonly held beliefs, approach the problem of access to content in slightly different ways.

Gold Open Access

Gold open access—or the so-called gold road to open access—or simply Gold OA, refers to those journals that publish peer-reviewed articles without paid subscription barriers for their readers. However, this does not mean that costs do not exist. Instead, costs are transferred to authors via article processing charges (APCs). The APCs are paid by authors, their parent institutions, or related grant-funding agencies. The process works to a surprisingly successful degree. Some of the most prominent journals in various disciplines are gold OA journals, including the *Public Library of Science*, *ArXiv*, *Annals of Family Medicine*, *Duke Law Review*, and more (Grumpenberger, Ovalle-Perandones, and Gorraiz 2013). Such gold OA journals have become the standard for their respective disciplines. Nevertheless, the financial burdens fall upon faculty or scholars, who may not necessarily have the funds to cover the APCs. In some cases APCs are exceedingly expensive—several thousands of dollars per article to pay for perpetual open access. These fee scales are sometimes unaffordable for authors or institutions reined in by smaller budgets.

107

Green Open Access

As a result of some of the financial issues regarding gold open access, green open access (or green OA) attempts to gather the earlier versions of works that have already been published. Most university institutional repositories collect the pre-print, print, and draft versions of the content created by their own faculty. The narrower scope—usually just focusing on the journal publications of individual faculty aligned with a university—affords a little more flexibility from publishers. In some cases, the green OA repository arose because online databases have priced out libraries and universities from accessing the very scholarship funded by them. It is seen, then, as a way for libraries to guarantee perpetual access to their institutions' own scholarship by circumventing the paywalls constructed by proprietary interests that also often have the original author's copyrights transferred to them as well.

Outcomes and Results of Open Access

Some publishers have been compliant with open access, but many have not. As a result, two sides have formed. One side is strongly in favor of open access; the other is just as strongly against open access. As Vincent and Wickham (2013) write, "The position that open access is ethically necessary and/or inevitable, and the position that it has so many practical problems attached to it that it risks being pointlessly destructive unless they are resolved, each seem the obvious starting-point to substantial groups of researchers." The two sides essentially do not take into account the validity of the other side's points.

The result of this lack of compromise is an escalating cycle in which one side continually increases prices to the point that only the richest can afford the service and/or content, whereas the ones that are priced out have to find content elsewhere. Those stuck in the middle wind up having to seek out more open access materials, settle for inferior products, drop other materials, or resort to various workarounds. As Gardner (2013) writes, "Learned societies suddenly found themselves caught, largely powerless, in the crossfire a battle between an evangelical RCUK/Wellcome Foundation [an OA group] and the commercial publishers over rising costs and profits."

However, even if open access is contributing to some of the issue of rising costs, the only existing safety valve to the issue of rising journal and subscription access costs is open access. If enough major organizations and governing bodies join the movement, publishers will have to compromise on their often draconian approaches to academic scholarly communication.

MDLs and Open Access Books: Bridge or Chasm?

The overall discussion of open access focuses mostly on journal publication. However, as table 8.1 shows, books are still an essential part of scholarly communication in certain disciplines. Open access, as a result of its intense focus on journals, has less of an impact on such disciplines, mostly in the humanities and social sciences.

In some ways, monographs are a difficult beast: they "blur the boundary between specialist academic publications and what publishers call the general or

TABLE 8.1

Breakdown of publication types by discipline

Discipline	Books	Chapters	Journal articles	Other
English	39	27	31	3
History	40	22	37	1
French	37	23	39	1
Philosophy	14	20	65	1
Sociology	22	10	64	3
Law	18	15	65	1
Politics	29	9	62	0
Economics	1	2	89	7
Chemistry	0	0	100	0

SOURCE: Vincent (2013).

trade list" (Vincent 2013). As a result, many special concessions made by journal editors, learned societies, and their publishers might not apply. Open access journals tend to be for limited audiences. However, monographs are often written and published with a wider audience in mind. As a result, there is much more revenue at stake with monograph titles than with journal articles. The potential for loss is much greater in terms of costs of labor, printing, and marketing such books. Providing open access books is much more problematic.

There are some strategies, however, that have been developed to help improve open access for books. In each of these solutions it might be possible for MDLs to play a large role in the development of such OA texts.

The first strategy involves posting books as PDFs on a website. This is not unlike what happens currently with scholarly articles. Faculty in certain science, technology, engineering and mathematics disciplines often post copies of their papers on personal websites. A similar action might be taken by authors of monographs interested in allowing their content to be accessible to anyone. Some institutions already allow access to long white papers, reports, and even published book-length documents (Vincent 2013). This type of model has become known as the platinum model of open access, in which OA publishing fees are charged to neither the author nor the reader. Instead, consortia work together to provide the economic sustainability to absorb costs. Some examples of these include Open Book Publishers and Knowledge Unlatched (Vincent 2013).

How might an MDL be incorporated into such a scheme? In many ways, the sheer size of MDLs predispose them to being very helpful for such publications. Users would be drawn by the sheer numbers of items already within the collection, much as they are already drawn to Google Search. As we have seen, MDLs also have consortia partners built into their collections. HathiTrust and Google Books have dozens of institutional partners each. The power of their cooperative forces could be gathered to create and support such platinum OA endeavors. Advertising revenue generated in the case of Google Books would alone support the publishing costs of the endeavor.

The second strategy would be to mimic the process of gold OA by charging authors or their funding institutions article-processing fees, but on a larger scale. In this case the APCs would range in the tens of thousands of dollars rather than a few hundred to several thousand dollars. MDLs would be able to provide records, a solid searchable system, and name recognition in order to improve the overall accessibility of the work.

Finally, the green open access strategy would work in ways similar to the current institutional repositories that collect the preprints, postprints, and occasional final versions of scholarly institutional-related papers. It would be easy enough to upload the drafted versions of a book into, for example, a DSpace system. As with many repositories, multiple versions of a document can be stored in a single record. This would allow users to access the information without the same formatting.

However, one issue with a green OA repository of e-books and monographs will be deciding upon an industry-standard period of embargo. Currently, many publishers of scholarly articles require embargoes of twelve to twenty-four months. This may prove much too short of a time for book-length subject treatments. It may be that a period of five to ten years would be sufficient for a publisher to receive enough revenue to support the endeavor. Beyond ten years would likely be an unreasonable amount of time, as the marketability of most copyrighted materials declines quickly (Schruers 2013). The 2003 case *Eldred v. Ashcroft* examined the constitutionality of the Copyright Term Extension Act (CTEA); the case cited a study of books examined that held renewed copyrights prior to the 1998 CTEA investigations, and only 11 percent had any commercial value.[3] Beyond a certain period of time, it appears that most books will not have any economic benefit for the copyright owners. The key is to find that sweet spot of how long to market the work for the maximum economic benefit and when to allow it to be freed from embargo.

It may be that MDLs can help with managing such embargo periods. Placing an item in the HathiTrust, for example—itself a highly searchable system with robust metadata—would also allow its author to have automated embargo terms or to limit users who have to authenticate to access the content. The HathiTrust already provides greater access to content for its members than to at-large users. Perhaps if a monograph or book were offered online as part of a university class, the class members might have limited access to it during the time when the book is embargoed.

MDLS' STRATEGIES TO PROVIDE AND LIMIT ACCESS

As described in the previous chapter on copyright, materials falling in the public domain are fully accessible. However, because of the lawsuits brought forth by the Authors Guild and others, MDLs will provide only limited access to works still operating under copyright law. As a result, most of the books in MDL collections are kept behind access walls. This section examines how Google Books, the HathiTrust, Europeana, and the Open Library limit access to digital books restricted by copyright. Although the Internet Archive doesn't upload books that are copyright protected, its access layout is worth examining and so is included in this chapter.

Google Books

Google Books controls access to the digital books in its MDL using the following four levels: record only, snippet view, partial view, and full view. Record-only view provides only the most basic metadata for a book and no possibility of seeing the text, in much the same way that libraries or OCLC's WorldCat do with their integrated library system online catalogs.

The information about the book itself includes as a minimum the following metadata elements in the order they appear in the online user interface:

- Title
- Author
- Edition (if applicable)
- Publisher
- ISBN (if applicable)
- Original from (source of the original book, such as New York Public Library)

- Digitized (date)
- Length (number of pages)
- Subjects (if applicable, selected from BISAC subjects)

Records also include the thumbnails of related books; table of contents; QR codes; customer reviews; star ratings; and links to citation manager software solutions such as BibTeX, EndNote, and RefMan. The record-only view is likely an indication that a book has not been placed into Google Books' digital corpus of books.

Along with this basic metadata, the higher levels of access—snippet, preview, and full text—provide varying levels of access to the digital text. The snippet view

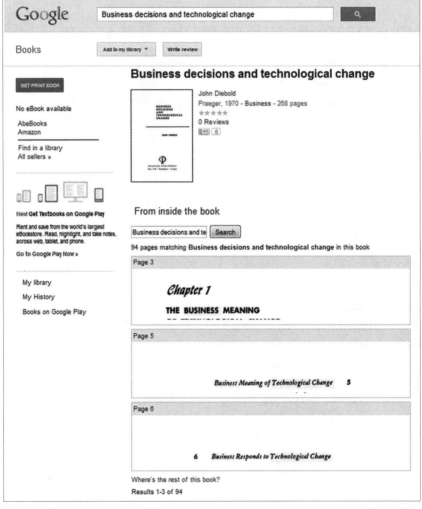

FIGURE 8.2
Google snippet view, which includes boxes
that provide a few sentence or words of highlighted text.

includes small boxes of text roughly two inches in length from top to bottom by five inches in width. As shown in figure 8.2, these snippets include a few sentences of the text along with queried keywords.

One can search the full text of the book and receive small segments of it to aid in research or other endeavors. However, Google is also careful to provide an explanation to users as to why the access is limited for the book. The text question "Where's the rest of this book?", which appears under a hyperlink, takes users to a page explaining access policies.

Google's policy is twofold. If an author is a Google partner, then the author is the one choosing the level of access. If an author is not a partner, then Google provides only a record or a snippet view. The policy states, "The aim of Google Books is to help you discover books and assist you with buying them or finding a copy at a local library. It's like going to a bookstore and browsing—with a Google twist."[4]

Preview access provides more of the text, allowing users to look at full pages within it, though still not at the whole text. In figure 8.3 one can see how the whole book is provided online, but certain pages are omitted. Google states just below the cover page that the amount of pages visible to readers will be limited.

In full view, all of the text is provided in open access to all readers. In its policy, Google states that "[its] partners decide how much of the book is browsable—anywhere from a few sample pages to the whole book. Some partners offer the entire

113

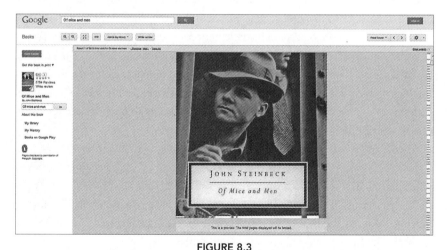

FIGURE 8.3
Preview view of Google Books, showing cover and
basic metadata along with the note "This is a preview.
The total pages displayed will be limited."

book in a digital edition through Google eBooks, in which case you can purchase the book."[5]

Google appears to be attempting to provide accessibility to readers as well as marketability for authors within its system. As for authors or copyright owners who choose to provide the book openly, this follows much of the same rationale as platinum open access.

As stated earlier, there may be longer-term benefits for publishers and authors to provide titles in an open access environment. MDLs not only provide information in monograph form to users but also stimulate interest in a topic or publisher imprint. The focus of Google Books appears to be more on the general population, that is, as a digital public library on a mass scale. As a result, the publishers of trade and general interest publications involved with Google Books would likely benefit the most. Yet as we will see in the following sections, such considerations of audience are different since the intended users for other MDLs are of a more academic or cultural nature.

HathiTrust

The HathiTrust's vision for its MDL has always been slightly different in scope and intent than the Google Books digitization project. While some may ascertain some questionable or at least profit-driven motives on the part of Google, the HathiTrust has taken great pains to avoid such legal entanglements. As a result of both its cautiousness relative to Google's and its basic nonprofit educational philosophy, access to content in the HathiTrust MDL is more restricted. Instead of the four possible levels of access, there are only two: limited view and full view. Since the individual catalogs of each consortium partner and OCLC's WorldCat already handle titles that are not digitized, the HathiTrust's MDL is meant only to provide access to texts that have been digitized.

HathiTrust is a much more uniform, accountable, and streamlined system as a result. It is easy to surmise whether HathiTrust has a digital version of a book, which affects user trust.

The advantage of the HathiTrust is its metadata, based on the robust cataloging practices of its member libraries. For each of the records, regardless of snippet or full view, the following access points are provided:

- Main author
- Other authors
- Language(s)
- Published (year)

- Note
- Physical description
- Original format
- Original classification number

Additionally, the HathiTrust lists "Locate a Print Version" as part of its item description, and links out to OCLC's WorldCat, which provides a list of the nearest libraries holding a physical copy of the work.

The limited view (see figure 8.4), similar to snippet view in Google Books, doesn't allow nonmember users to see the text. The text itself, however, is searchable so that users might be able to infer whether the text had the types of information that they were looking for. The approach is a conservative one in several ways. It prevents outside users from "stealing" text. It protects copyright but also allows users to at least access some of the intellectual content of the source materials without shutting them out completely. Yet it is also a somewhat unsatisfying search experience for many users. It is questionable if matching queried keywords will provide the typical user with what he or she needs. It is also questionable

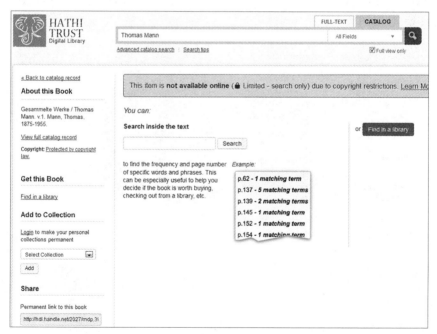

FIGURE 8.4
HathiTrust's limited view and "search inside the text" function,
for users to determine frequency of sought-after information.

whether such limitations also predetermine one's fair use rights, much like digital rights management in music has been criticized, as one's actions are curtailed even before one can try to use information. One is locked out before one can even try to apply the fair use doctrine to a text within the HathiTrust.

The full view of the HathiTrust items allows users to access any part of the text. HathiTrust's policy to bundle related files together like many institutional repositories is a significant improvement over the mishmash of records that Google Books provides users. This ability to provide access to multiple volumes through one access point improves findability.

The accessibility of these full texts is also limited, though. Only members of a partner institution can have access to downloadable PDF files. At-large users are restricted to browsing the texts on their online e-reader software. Sometimes this is sufficient. However, people who have a slow Internet connection or older computer, or who are missing the requisite software, will not be able to view the texts in a satisfactory manner. Furthermore, although controls exist to allow users to zoom or turn pages or refresh, text loading is time consuming and the user interface is awkward (see figure 8.5). To take full advantage of the texts, one must also have a large screen to be able to read the text.

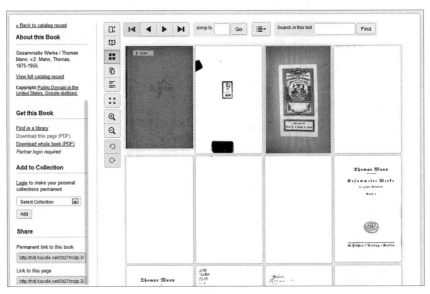

FIGURE 8.5
HathiTrust's full view, showing its online e-text reader
in thumbnail page view and its user-interface controls.

Overall, the display allows users to get a sense of the text and to read not only the PDF original version but also, if one prefers, the OCR text only. Users can also search, view in full pages, zoom in and out, and rotate pages left or right.

Europeana

Europeana's mission is to advocate for a stronger and more robust public domain. One of its strategies for strengthening the public domain is to work with Creative Commons licensing. This allows authors to predetermine copyrights so that end users and consumers can judge quickly and easily whether or not they can use a work for various purposes.

Although Google Books provides a partnership program for authors, it does not necessarily reflect a reliance on the Creative Commons movement. In many ways, as is often the case with Google, the project remains opaque, and it is unclear how many books are actually in the Google Books corpus. Europeana, however, appears willing to embrace international standards of cooperation such as the Creative Commons license.

Access to works licensed with Creative Commons is provided in ways similar to the HathiTrust, with some works available in limited view and others available in full text. A brief search for public domain works in the Europeana corpus yielded about two million results, a sizable collection of materials for users.

Open Library

The Open Library markets its service as "a record for every book." As a result, its catalog contains millions of records for books in the same way that OCLC's World-Cat does. However, it also allows users to access its digitized full-text works. As a result, accessibility is limited to two types: record only and full text. The record-only view provides basic metadata similar to Google Books. It is somewhat sparse with the presentation of the metadata. In the example shown in figure 8.6, the author is listed under the heading "people." It also provides a blurb for describing the text and a table providing all of the available editions.

There are seventy-five editions of Goethe's *Egmont* available. The table then provides a link to the various file formats, if available, and tells users how they can use the content: read, borrow, or buy.

The full-text view provides some interesting variations from other MDLs, however. First, the project provides a full-text option for any item that is in the

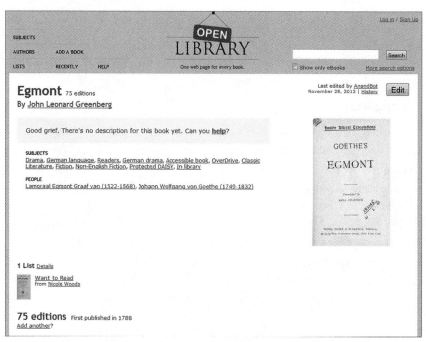

FIGURE 8.6
View of the Open Library record for *Egmont,*
by Johann Wolfgang von Goethe.

public domain. Users can download or view in an online reader in various formats, including PDF HTML text markup, ePub, DjVu, MOBI and Kindle.

The hyperlinks often leave the Open Library domain to other MDLs, including the Internet Archive. Full access is also provided to disabled users via the Digital Accessible Information System (DAISY) format. The Americans with Disabilities Act often trumps concerns about copyright and allows users who are Open Library community members and who have registered DAISY accounts with accepted services such as the National Library Service (NLS) for the Blind and Physically Handicapped to access the texts. There are also open DAISY titles for anyone to use. Overall, the concern for people with disabilities to access texts is Open Library's greatest strength.

Internet Archive

The Internet Archive lists as its policy uploading only those books that are in the public domain.[6] As a result, there is only one level of accessibility in the system: full view. Searches for various texts that might yield records, snippets, or partial views

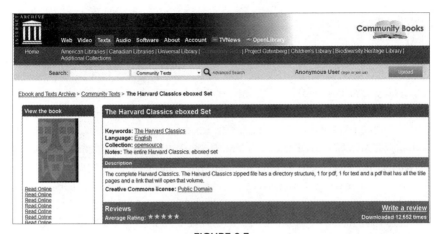

FIGURE 8.7
Screenshot of the Internet Archive showing "The Harvard Classics eboxed set," all fifty-one of the set's digitized volumes in one record.

in the other MDLs yield nothing in the Internet Archive. The collection is therefore 100 percent open access, but it is limited in the number of texts available. This limitation is also one of its strengths. When users find something in the Internet Archive, they can know with great certainty that it is available for download and immediate use.

Users are able to acquire the content in the Internet Archive in a number of different ways. First, users can view the book online, and they can choose various file formats (e.g., PDFs, EPUBs, Kindle, Daisy, HTML OCR text, DjVU). All files are held on the server in one HTTPS index location as well. Metadata elements are provided for users, including author, subject, publisher, language, call numbers, digitization sponsors, and book contributors. Also included are technical metadata regarding the scanning equipment, policies, image parameters (e.g., PPI, OCR), and more. The robust metadata in the Internet Archive is far superior to that of Google Books and of the Open Library in terms of access points and rivals that of the HathiTrust. Even multiple files and volumes are occasionally bundled, as seen in the example in figure 8.7, although this is not applied uniformly to all titles in the Internet Archive as it is in the HathiTrust.

CONCLUSION

Access levels vary greatly with MDLs. On the one hand, open access in its varieties could easily be integrated into various MDLs, depending on their missions. Open access would surely raise the profile of many works that are currently locked or restricted by copyright. Platinum OA might be implemented by creating fee-supporting bodies out of current MDL consortia members. HathiTrust, with its implicit and explicit focus on academia, might be the best candidate for such a publishing endeavor. Gold OA could also be integrated with MDLs in much the same way, though it would be more successful with scaled article processing fees (APCs). Green OA would be possible to implement as well, but much longer embargo terms would have to be implemented to reflect the higher costs and longer periods of time needed to recoup publication expenses.

On the other hand, MDLs—as determined in the 2012 case *Authors Guild v. HathiTrust*—must respect the rights of the author of the source material.[7] To do so, all MDLs have developed system features or overall content gathering policies that limit some visibility or acquisition of the text. Google Books is the least restrictive with its four levels of access; the more conservative HathiTrust provides two levels of access; Europeana provides open access to public domain works; Internet Archive provides one view only (full text of public domain materials); and the Open Library provides two levels as well. Open Library also allows community users to log in to access a limited amount of texts. At the same time it provides access to those with disabilities by offering both open and protected DAISY reader versions of texts.

Overall, access is being navigated by each of the MDLs in different ways. Although complete open access with MDLs will likely never happen, their philosophies generally overlap with the basic tenets of the OA movement. Perhaps if copyright laws loosen a bit with regard to digitized books, especially with orphan works, MDLs will be able to provide an even greater amount of open access.

REFERENCES

Gardner, Rita. 2013. "Open Access and Learned Societies." In *Debating Open Access*, ed. Nigel Vincent and Chris Wickham. London: British Academy. www.britac.ac.uk/openaccess/debatingopenaccess.cfm.

Grumpenberger, Christian, María-Antonia Ovalle-Perandones, and Juan Gorraiz. 2013. "On the Impact of Gold Open Access Journals." *Scientometrics* 96, no. 1: 221–38.

Schruers, Matt. 2013. How Long Can Copyright Holders Wait to Sue? *Disruptive Competition Project*. www.project-disco.org/intellectual-property/100313-how-long-can-copyright-holders-wait-to-sue/.

Vincent, Nigel. 2013. "The Monograph Challenge." In *Debating Open Access*, ed. Nigel Vincent and Chris Wickham. London: British Academy. www.britac.ac.uk/openaccess/debatingopenaccess.cfm.

Vincent, Nigel, and Chris Wickham. 2013. Introduction to *Debating Open Access*, ed. Nigel Vincent and Chris Wickham. London: British Academy. www.britac.ac.uk/openaccess/debatingopenaccess.cfm.

NOTES

1. Ian Sample, "Harvard University Says It Can't Afford Journal Publishers' Prices," *Guardian*, April 24, 2012, www.theguardian.com/science/2012/apr/24/harvard-university-journal-publishers-prices.

2. "Sticker Shock 2: Cost-Per-Use," Cornell University, http://engineering.library.cornell.edu/about/stickershock_stats.

3. Eldred v. Ashcroft, 538 U.S. 916 (2003).

4. "Why Some Books Aren't Available in Full-Text," Google Books, https://support.google.com/books/answer/43729?topic=9259&hl=en.

5. Ibid.

6. Internet Archive Digital Library, https://archive.org/about/faqs.php.

7. Authors Guild v. HathiTrust, 902 F.Supp.2d 445, 104 U.S.P.Q.2d 1659, Copyr.L.Rep. ¶ 30327 (October 10, 2012).

Part 3

Practical Applications

Chapter Nine

Using MDLs in Libraries— or, To What End?

M uch of the discussion thus far has focused on the theoretical, philosophical, and systemic foundations of massive digital libraries (MDLs). The use of MDLs in real library settings for actual library patrons is something that needs to be addressed, and it is one of the main reasons for this book. Currently, libraries tend to use Google Books or the HathiTrust—or any open content for that matter—as supplements to existing print collections, online subscription databases, and e-book licensing agreements. This chapter examines how libraries use MDLs in pragmatic ways to help enhance user experience and to harness the tendency of many people—students in particular—to rely solely on open web services such as Google Search and Google Scholar.

SUPPLEMENTING PRINT COLLECTIONS WITH MDLS

"My (Public Domain) Library" and Hybrid Print-on-Demand Models

Without a doubt, the most exciting part of MDLs is the mass digitization of public domain works. This large corpus of openly available books helps libraries make more difficult choices when it comes to collection development. As of October 20, 2013, the HathiTrust contained 3,474,965 public domain volumes, or roughly 32 percent of its total. The Internet Archive contains nearly a million works in its collections, all of which are in the public domain. These files are downloadable in multiple file formats via HTTP as well as in BitTorrent, a faster downloadable format.[1]

It would be of use for a library to supply links to these public domain books in records found in their online catalogs to patrons who might not know that they exist. A public domain work could be part of any library's online catalog collection, much like e-journals are considered part of a library collection despite that they are physically located somewhere else. Indeed, as reported in the *Chronicle of Higher Education*, libraries are considering just that: "Mass-digitization projects, notably the creation of the HathiTrust digital repository with its nearly 11 million volumes, have also encouraged libraries to act. . . . If electronic copies of monographs exist, that takes some pressure off libraries to have print copies of them close by" (Howard 2013).

Along the same lines, another practical approach to using the public domain content found in MDLs might be to provide patrons with an open access e-reader "bookshelf" with all of the possible titles available for tablet readers, including the iPad, the Nook, and other platforms. Google Books' My Library service (see figure 9.1) allows users to develop their own library in this manner. A library—whether it be academic, public, or special—might consider creating its own "My Library" page that lists all the public domain books related to subjects that are useful for the various disciplines or areas of interest that most utilize such texts. For example, if a librarian at California State University, Northridge, creates a "My CSUN Public Domain Library" Google Books page, users might be able to browse open access and public domain titles, which they could then download or read on portable electronic devices.

But some people still prefer physical books. It would be of use, then, for some libraries to offer printing and bindery services for public domain works available from MDLs. In tandem with new library-sponsored digital publishing imprints, libraries could print such public domain works as a service to their patrons as well as to recoup money for their journals.

This kind of hybrid approach—essentially print-on-demand for patrons via an easy to use selection user interface—would provide a service that might not be found anywhere else. Libraries might be able to turn a slight profit doing this as well by printing books and binding them cheaply. As more and more libraries enter publishing with their institutional repositories or with such open source projects like the Open Journal Systems, such methods of recouping expenses, especially if professors are assigning classic texts for their classes, might be warranted.

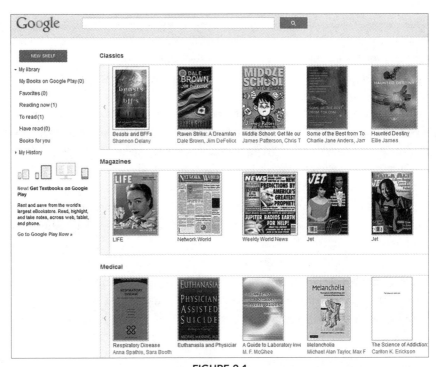

FIGURE 9.1
Google's My Library can be used to help library patrons
keep track of books on a library's own virtual digital bookshelves.

A current project that provides this very service is McNally Jackson Books' Public Domain Print-on-Demand service.[2] Searching within available public domain titles on their site for "Shakespeare" brings a list of candidate titles to print. Generally, the price ranges from $8.99 to $19.00. This is somewhat reasonable, though not as cheap as one might think. On the same note, if a library prints out a public domain book at $5.00 per title, or some other low but manageable fee, it might save money for students while helping a library generate funds toward open access or other in-house publishing initiatives.

Access and Print Preservation

The digital copy of a print book eliminates much of the wear and tear that occurs when patrons handle books. In the case of most books kept in a library's general collection or stacks, this is not always necessary. However, in the case of out-of-print, rare, or damaged books—especially those that appear in special collections and archives—less physical handling and more virtual access is preferable. In these cases, if a book is too rare to touch but exists in one of the many MDLs, one might be better able to not only preserve the in-house work but also provide full access to the content.

Taking things a step further, if a library holds a number of rare books that fall within the public domain, it might be worthwhile for that library to partner with the Internet Archive or other MDLs to create a larger audience for the work. One can digitize one's own books and have them uploaded to the Internet Archive without too much trouble. Later, one could improve access as well as preserve the physical version. Some libraries are currently doing this. In particular, Cornell University has provided access to about eighty thousand books in partnership with the Internet Archive.[3]

Additionally, sometimes libraries' in-house versions of rare texts are damaged or rendered illegible because of environmental conditions or misuse. It might be useful to use the versions found online in MDLs to supplement in-house versions or to provide users with a better version.

Aggregation of Variant Texts

At the same time, it might also be useful for archives, historians, or even bibliophiles to combine multiple versions of the texts found online to create collated "superversions" of a text that incorporate all variances. Scholars might use MDLs as editorial tools to help create new, definitive versions of old texts. What was done in the previous centuries for the collation of sacred texts, including the New Testament, for example, could be done more quickly if all the variant texts were digitized, placed online, and immediately findable. The seemingly redundant digitization of the same title might in these cases be a boon to scholars. "Aggregated texts" might be a new direction for digital humanities and could give new life to outdated editions of works.

DECIDING TO PHASE OUT OR WEED PRINT COLLECTIONS

It's never an easy decision to reduce items from a library. Relevance and currency always play a role, but space always winds up being the most important consideration. However, digital access has allowed libraries to downsize collections more easily. This section examines how MDLs can positively affect decision making when deciding what to do with print collections.

Weeding Projects

Many libraries need to conduct weeding projects now more than ever. Shrinking "real estate" in buildings is a growing phenomenon. Currently, for example, the library at California State University, Northridge (CSUN), is undergoing weeding projects as a result of the remodeling and renovation of the library and the addition of a new learning commons modeled center and an outside student writing center. As result, real estate devoted to the stacks has decreased immensely. The library will be removing nearly one hundred thousand volumes from its collection over the next few years.

Weeding at CSUN is being conducted by looking at usage statistics, times checked out, times requested from the automated storage and retrieval system (ASRS), and times reshelved. None of these approaches is necessarily perfect. It is not always clear if users were able to get what they wanted. Users don't leave a "satisfied" or "found what I wanted" note on the inside covers of the books! Instead, librarians need to extrapolate from numerous uses. If a book has been checked out once a year, it may demonstrate significant usage. If it was checked out once in twenty years, perhaps there is really not much interest in the book.

At the same time, using electronic theses and dissertations as an example, we can see that current methods for determining usage are inadequate at best. At CSUN one thesis published in 2001, "An Analysis of Gustav Holst's *The Planets*," by Kanokrut Leelasiri, was checked out three times in the twelve years since it was published. In October 2012, the thesis was digitized and placed online in CSUN's open access institutional repository ScholarWorks. Unexpectedly, from October 2012 to October 2013 the thesis file was downloaded more than 1,400 times, and its ScholarWorks metadata record was viewed more than eight hundred times. In a Google Search for "holst planets analysis" as the search terms, the link to the PDF appears first in the retrieved set results; the link to a record in Google Books appears about twelfth. What becomes clear is that a book on a shelf not only has a more limited audience but also is subject to hidden physical actions that cannot be monitored. The thesis may have been browsed numerous times each semester, but it was not possible to track that action.

Following the same reasoning, a way for librarians to make better decisions about weeding might be through reliance on the digital version found in the MDL.

If a large number of users are accessing a particular text online, perhaps that text would be worth saving—especially if local usage statistics are inconclusive. In the case of the thesis already mentioned, given its usage online, it might now be worth it to keep extra physical copies. Perhaps if the book were accessed online from somewhere else, not locally, it would show that particular subjects might not be strong or popular at a particular institution. In this way, if usage statistics from MDLs could be publicly accessible to libraries, perhaps they would help librarians make a case for saving or not saving a book in the local collection.

At the same, one might argue that if a book appears online this is cause to remove it from the collection. However, principles of library and information science are still paramount. Local statistics and user needs still need to be taken into account before weeding. If a book were purchased to supplement a particular course and that course was no longer taught, then it would be important to look at overall statistics of the book's use. If the book is used heavily worldwide, then perhaps it should stay. If the book is not used by anyone anywhere, including locally, then it might be easier to make the decision to weed it as well.

Just in Time versus Just in Case

The library world is currently shifting from the traditional just-in-case collection development philosophy, in which libraries provide copies of things even if there's no explicitly stated need for them, to the just-in-time, or on-demand, approach, in which libraries use patron demand as the justification for purchase. Libraries are looking to adopt models that provide content based on stated long-tail needs rather than by buying resources on the off chance that someone might want to use them someday.

MDLs may help fill this new model of patron driven acquisition in cost-effective ways. If a library receives a request for material to purchase, libraries might consider relying on an MDL to see if the work is available online for a user. The MDL would be one more of a number of supplemental access points to allow users the ability to read or take advantage of a work. At the same time, relying on the digital access would only be part of the picture. Surely if a book were requested by a department and the funds were available, it might be more prudent to purchase the book, especially when dealing with patrons or faculty who prefer the physical object to the digital facsimile.

However, issues arise when a book is placed on course reserves. If one copy of a book exists, then it might be useful to make use of an MDL if the book is in the public domain. Numerous users would be able to access a version of the text if it was placed on reserve and another patron was using it.

The issue of demand also applies when books or resources are checked out from the library. A library is not always able to provide several copies of a work. If it does, it often is the case that one copy is worn out and others are in perfect condition. By relying on MDLs, libraries might be able to do away with the multiple-copy just-in-case model as well. Yet some libraries appear to be reluctant to go this route. Many fear that students will bypass the whole library and use Google primarily for everything. In some ways this is a fairly common sentiment. All channels that used to run through the library now have alternate routes. Libraries and librarians are no longer primary gatekeepers of information, and updates to copyright law may make the library's standing as sharer of information resources even shakier.

However, this fear has proved mostly unwarranted. As Bourg writes, "Fears that students would abandon libraries and library collections in favor of whatever they could find online don't seem to be coming to fruition. . . . Students seem to be using Google Books to supplement their library research."[4] Let us hope that Google Books remains accessible for the long term. Fans of some of Google's older, phased-out services such as Meebo (discontinued in 2013), Google Wave (discontinued in 2010), and even Google Answers (discontinued in the Dark Ages of 2006), might still be feeling the sting and regret of relying on a for-profit company for long-term sustainability.

REAL-WORLD APPLICATIONS

Online Catalog Integration via Google Books API

Libraries can use Google Books to integrate their integrated library system (ILS) with online open access texts by adopting the Google Books API (application programming interface). One example, shown in figure 9.2, is available for view in the Oviatt Library's (CSUN) online catalog. A record in the library's Millennium ILS shows the cover of a book, as well as a button linking out to the record in Google Books. This enhanced ILS record will allow students to read a book directly that the library may have without having to examine its contents at the stacks. Sometimes, if a book is checked out, the student might be able to access this book in Google Books and read it this way. This feature is yet another way to help students access a book prior to coming to the library as well. Overall, the use of the system provides

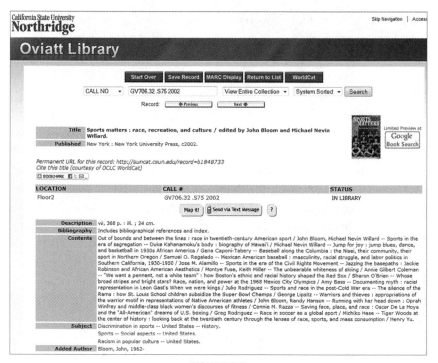

FIGURE 9.2
Screenshot of CSUN catalog showing icon linking
to a limited preview of the book in Google Book Search.

another useful service and access point for students. This system works best with public domain books. A student can browse the online catalog, see a few pages (or the whole thing) in Google Books, examine it on the shelf, and then check it out if he or she wants to.

The JavaScript coding for the Google API is not particularly difficult either. Upon receiving a valid response from Google, JavaScript generates a URL for the book record within Google Books. It then inserts the URL into a <DIV> section in the ILS's HTML page coding:

```
<div id=google style="font-size:9px;margin-left:4px;">
<span class="book-title" align="center"></span>
</div>
```

The JavaScript queries the Google Books database for a matching book title. If one has a view to provide, it appears in the online catalog.[5]

This enhancement of the library catalog is a very practical use for a MDL. It allows libraries to make use of some freely available content by integrating current library systems with users more typical online search behavior.

MDLs as a Tool for Research in the Digital Humanities

In some cutting-edge studies Michel and colleagues (2011) are mining the publicly available data sets from Google Books to "track the use of words over time, compare related words and even graph them." Their research involves examining the frequency with which words appear over time. One example the researchers found was that the number of references to men compared to the number of references to women in the Google Books digital corpus shows that men were referred to much more for centuries. By 1985, though, women had finally reached the same amount of mention as men. Since then, women have remained higher than men (Michel et al. 2011).

The purpose of data mining is to help researchers find trends in what people were writing about at particular points in history. As a result, the MDL becomes an extremely useful tool for historical, analytical research. The same kind of research can also be attempted using the HathiTrust search interface, which provides a list of the number of times a word appears in a book. Libraries can provide access as well as context and leadership among disciplines by simultaneously providing links and caveats about the usage of MDLs. It is clear that MDLs such as Google Books, Europeana, and HathiTrust would be useful tools for researching large bodies of digital literature.

Michel and colleagues (2011) examined 5,195,769 books, which is approximately 4 percent of all books printed, according to some estimates. Though about one-third the size of the current Google Books corpus, their sample is nevertheless a small fraction of the estimated 125 million printed books in the world. As a result of the small sample, variations and fluctuations may occur. It is often unclear— and Google hasn't fully disclosed this—just how many texts are actually available online and how many more may be missing. If the researchers searched through an incomplete record, perhaps there is a significant margin of error in their results. Furthermore, the Google Books corpus does not include newsprint, maps, or other non-monographic materials, which account for a sizable part of all libraries.

The print monograph record can surely be used as an aggregate mirror to peek into the culture as a whole, but one must not forget that it is still one slice of a larger mass, some of which—such as physical experience, unrecorded experience, spoken word, so-called deviant and/or censored material, illegal "black market" material—may never be captured officially in digital formats. Additionally, works subjected to OCR software are occasionally still illegible if the fonts are of an unusual kind or if other conditions alter the paper or ink quality.

CULTUROMICS AND LIBRARIES: THE GOOGLE BOOKS N-GRAM VIEWER

The result of Michel and colleagues' (2011) study has been increased interest in what they have dubbed "culturomics," an approach that relies on "massive, multi-institutional and multi-national consortia[,] . . . novel technologies enabling the assembly of vast datasets . . . and . . . the deployment of sophisticated computational and quantitative methods."[6]

Users are especially benefited by the search and data-mining capabilities of searching Google Books using the Google Books N-gram Viewer. This is a useful tool not only for historians, writers, artists, and social scientists, but also for libraries.

In the first example, shown in figure 9.3, a search involving the terms *Hiroshima* and *Nagasaki* was conducted. The search results show the frequency with which the words appeared in the English language, both British and American, during the

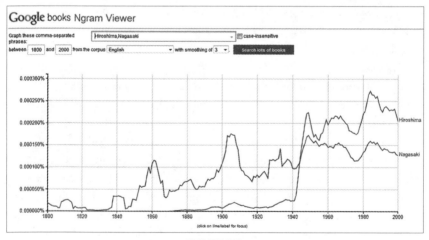

FIGURE 9.3
Ngram viewer showing frequency of the words *Hiroshima* and *Nagasaki* from 1800 to 2000 (note significant change starting in the early 1940s and spiking post–World War II).

period 1800–2000. For the first 140 years, "Nagasaki" was the more mentioned of the two cities, likely because it was the only port open to foreign trade during the Tokugawa era, a period in Japan known as *sakoku*. During the 1850s and 1860s, the city of Nagasaki began to surge, likely a result of the United States' aggressive policies to "open" up the country to international trade. Again, a surge occurred between 1900 and 1910, reflecting Nagasaki's status as a major hub for coal production and the winter port for the Russian Asiatic fleet until 1903.

The word "Hiroshima" during this same period of time was not mentioned very much in comparison, at a very distant second. However, during the years after the bombing of Pearl Harbor, Hiroshima was ever more frequently mentioned. Only by 1944, a year before the atomic bombings of both cities, had Hiroshima and Nagasaki reached parity in terms of frequency. After 1945 until the present day, as a result of being the first city to suffer an atomic bomb attack, Hiroshima has been mentioned the most. The interesting thing about this is that one can track historical events in the news or the ideas that accompany them. The N-Gram Viewer is truly a wonderful tool for researchers interested in the history of ideas and how events shape them. It is also a useful tool for students to get a better sense of the context of historical events and an understanding of how notoriety waxes and wanes over time.

Along with providing links to Google Books in the online public access catalog, libraries might also consider providing data visualizations of the search terms used by the library patrons to help with the frequency of terms being used. For example, say a student is interested in studying the history of the atomic bomb and is interested in Japanese history as it relates to that subject. Students could be provided a list of the terms that might be used to find something. The date ranges and frequencies of appearance for each search term might provide students with the starting point for their research. Looking again at figure 9.3, we can see that Hiroshima's notoriety began in the 1940s. Students would be able to understand the changes in graph and begin searching for materials within that time frame even if they were not that familiar with the history. There were also lulls in the discussion of these cities, especially in the periods 1954–60 and 1969–79. There are spikes in interest from 1962–68 and 1980–90. Students could be aided in their search for materials by being more aware of the periods of time in which a topic was discussed more often.

Libraries might also be able to use such metrics in terms of subjects to help determine whether books that discuss such subjects are nearing obsolescence, and then they would have quantitative data to back up their decision. For example, if

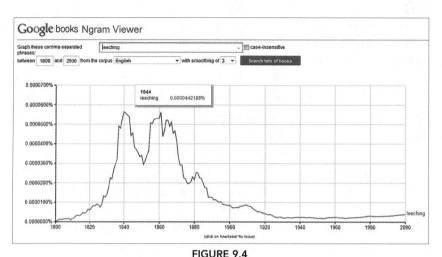

FIGURE 9.4

Google Ngram graph showing the frequency of mentions of the medical procedure known as leeching from 1800 to 2010 (note slight upturn in the 2000s as the procedure was found to be effective).

one takes a medical practice such as leeching (see figure 9.4), a procedure often represented as a naive and barbaric practice in the twentieth century, one might see some interesting data and conclude that perhaps the library might not want to discard or weed any books related to leeching.

Although nowhere near the historical heights from the 1850s, one can see in figure 9.5 that mention of the term "leeching" has increased by nearly three times from its historical low in 1954 (.0000017 percent) by of the year 2008 (.0000049 percent). In some circles, leeching is making a comeback as a viable medical procedure for some healing purposes (Wang 2011). The point is that libraries can make use of the jargon being used in specific disciplines to help in the collection development and weeding process.

Finally, libraries might be able to track the popularity of multimedia formats as they appear within the corpus as well. In the following example (figure 9.6), a search was run including various format acronyms, including VHS, MOV, MP3, streaming, and more. What was found were general increases in such digital formats as streaming video, MOV, and MP3 files, but an overall decline in the VHS format and—despite breakneck adoption in the 1990s and 2000s—a recent decline in DVDs. Perhaps a look at how people are mentioning formats in discourse can help one predict if a format will be thrown onto the dustbin of history once and for all or will persist over time. Although this is an uncontrolled result, it can nevertheless provide a sense of general trends.

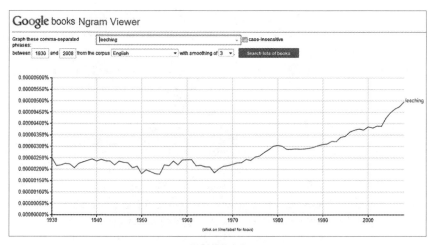

FIGURE 9.5
Google Ngram graph showing the frequency of leeching
mentioned between the years 1930 and 2010.

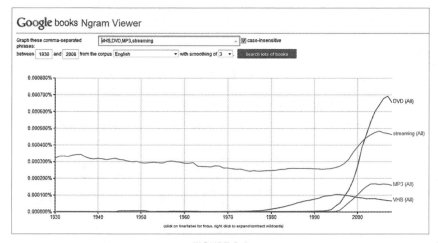

FIGURE 9.6
Google Ngram showing the frequency of various digital and analog formats
(including DVD, streaming, MP3, VHS) from 1930 to 2008.

CONCLUSION

It is clear from the various tools and services highlighted in this chapter that the
data and the information provided by various MDLs not only is valuable to users
but also is of practical use for all libraries. In particular, libraries with strained
budgets, shrinking sizes, or even expanding their scope on stagnant budgets can

do so without resorting to drastic measures. Libraries can take advantage of the great number of public domain books available. Libraries can also become more proactive in anticipating the needs of users by examining the metrics found in the Google Books corpus. Overall, the practical uses available from MDLs are robust, and users and librarians alike will be able to take advantage of them.

REFERENCES

Howard, Jennifer. 2013. "Short on Space, Libraries Look to One Another for Solutions." *Chronicle of Higher Education*, October 7. http://chronicle.com/article/Short-on-Space -Libraries-Look/142145/?cid=at&utm_source=at&utm_medium=en.

Michel, Jean-Baptiste, Yuan Kui Shen, Aviva Presser Aiden, Adrian Veres, Matthew K. Gray, Joseph P. Pickett, Dale Hoiberg, Dan Clancy, Peter Norvig, Jon Orwant, Steven Pinker, and Erez Lieberman Aiden. 2011. "Quantitative Analysis of Culture Using Millions of Digitized Books." *Science* 331, no. 6014: 176–82.

Wang, Joanna. 2011. "Medicinal Leeches: Nature's Finest Surgical Tool from the Swamps." *Yale Journal of Medicine and Law* 7, no. 3 (August 8). www.yalemedlaw .com/2011/08/medicinal-leeches-natures-finest-surgical-tool-from-the-swamps/.

NOTES

1. Lee Kaelin, "The Internet Archive Offers 1m+ Public Domain Works via BitTorrent," *TechSpot*, August 9, 2012, www.techspot.com/news/49694-the-internet-archive -offers-1m-public-domain-works-via-bittorrent.html.

2. "Public Domain Print on Demand," www.mcnallyjackson.com/print-on-demand/ public-domain.

3. "Cornell University Library Partners with the Internet Archive," Cornell University, http://news.library.cornell.edu/content/cornell-university-library-partners-internet -archive.

4. Chris Bourg, "How Students Use Google Books," *Feral Librarian* (blog), March 30, 2009, http://chrisbourg.wordpress.com/2009/03/30/how-students-use-google-books/.

5. Email correspondence with Eric Willis, library systems administrator, California State University, Northridge, July 22, 2013.

6. "FAQs," Culturomics, www.culturomics.org/Resources/faq.

Chapter Ten

Four MDL Studies

As for the future, your task is not to foresee it, but to enable it.

—Antoine de St. Exupery

This chapter provides four studies that evaluate massive digital libraries (MDLs). While primarily focusing on Google Books, currently the largest of the MDLs, these studies, outlined here by Ryan James (studies 1–3) and Andrew Weiss (study 4), are intended to be a practical starting point for the development of analytical approaches to MDLs. Each study focuses on different aspects of an MDL. In study 1, the issue of legibility of the scanned books in Google Books is examined. In study 2, metadata accuracy is analyzed. Study 3 examines the issues of culture and diversity in MDLs. Finally, study 4 provides an analysis of a cross-cultural, international partnership between Keio University in Tokyo and the American-based Google Books.

Each study is meant to provide practical approaches and theoretical foundations to assessing the worth of the digital collections with MDLs. It is hoped that other researchers will use these as starting points for more comprehensive studies as well as begin to formulate better theoretical and conceptual approaches with strong grounding in information and computer science.

Ryan James contributed to this chapter.

STUDY 1

LEGIBILITY OF GOOGLE BOOKS

One of the concerns raised early in the development of MDLs was the quality of the scanned images they were producing. Duguid in 2007 suggested that the poor quality of scanned books would not be as useful to scholars as an original physical book.[1] The benefits of access to a large number of books through MDLs would be reduced by poor proxies of the original book. His method was to closely scrutinize the scans of one book. While this method is useful for understanding the types of errors one might find, it tells us nothing of their prevalence. There was no way for Duguid to say if a chosen book had above or below the average number of errors.

This is, of course, an important aspect to consider: a library full of unreadable books is likely to not be of very much use to its patrons. To investigate this question it was decided to randomly sample a number of books from Google Books and inspect their pages for quality issues (James 2010). The unit of analysis—the item being studied—was the individual pages themselves, not any given book as a whole or even a group of books. This approach gave rise to methodological problems. Books are not of uniform page length and do not contain the same amount of characters. Also, as a metric, quality control contains subjective aspects that make it difficult to quantify.

Ideally, one would be able to randomly select a page from all available pages to inspect them. However, with the Google Books interface this is not possible. The compromise was to randomly select a book and then inspect a certain number of pages. Because books vary in length, it was decided to examine the first fifty pages of each book chosen, excluding the prefatory material, such as title page and table of contents.

Selecting a random book was further complicated by the fact that Google Books assigns unique identifiers to each book but does not publicly explain how it does so or what the identifiers' numerical ranges are. The solution settled on was to randomly select a word from the *Oxford English Dictionary*, input it in Google Books to generate a results list, and then randomly select one of the books from the results list. This second level of randomization is key, because we do not know how Google orders the results list. We simply cannot take the first result from the list because Google displays the results list based on its own relevance-ranking algorithms that attempt to approximate the perceived popularity of a given text. That text, because of its "popularity," might have been given extra scrutiny during whatever quality control phase Google implemented.

Once a book was selected, the next problem was to define legibility. Broadly defined, legibility is a text's capability of being read or deciphered. Because people have different abilities to read text on page, it was not possible to come up with a metric that could be easily operationalized. Instead, it was decided to focus on major errors, such as portions of the text that were completely unreadable by anyone, and minor errors, such as portions of the text that were difficult to read.

Major errors were easier to define than minor ones. Examples of major errors found included Google employees' accidentally scanning a page while their hand covered part of the text and scanning pages while they were in the process of turning them so that two or more pages overlapped, leaving all pages unreadable. The minor errors were more subjective. The idea was to find text blocks with errors that the user could still read but only with considerable effort. In focus were blurred text, missing letters from a sizable number of words, and contrast and resolution problems.

In total, 2,500 pages from fifty randomly selected books were examined. Approximately 1 percent of the pages had either major or minor errors. While this means that Google Books is not perfect, most pages examined were legible. This of course will not be very comforting to patrons who discover an error while reading a book central to their scholarship. To people reading for leisure, this might not be such a problem, except of course if the error is on the page that tells them if the butler did it.

The sample size led to concerns that it might be too small to give an accurate estimate of the average number of errors. A larger sample would have been preferable, but there was a limited amount of time that could be devoted to the project. The estimate of error rates was thus labeled a "preliminary result" to avoid disagreements with the peer reviewers.

McEathron (2010) conducted a similar study with a larger sample size. He randomly selected 180 books on geology from the HathiTrust and then examined all of their pages, some 47,287 pages in total. The result was that 2.5 percent of pages had errors. On the surface this suggests that the original 1 percent error rate for Google Books might have been an underestimate, but 65 percent of errors McEathron found came from one book. If we subtract these errors as an outlier, the final number is 0.875 percent, very close to 1 percent. McEathron, in an email to Ryan James, said such a large sample size was difficult to process (i.e., extremely tedious), and he was unlikely to conduct a similar such large scale study.

Although Google Books and the HathiTrust do not have the exact same corpus, many of the books scanned by Google are in both MDLs, and the other books were likely scanned under similar circumstances. Following this reasoning, the results are comparable. The data suggests that other MDLs may have a similar legibility error rate of around 1 percent.

The good news for this low figure is that books in the Google Books and HathiTrust MDLs appear to have few errors that affect the ability of a user to read them. The bad news may be a little harder to conceptualize. What would be the result if we let a child draw on 1 percent of all the pages in all the world's books with a crayon? Some information would be lost, with unreadable pages. Some we might still be able to decipher, but there would be a loss of some knowledge that might be irretrievable. Given the number of books available and the amount of information they contain, this loss would nevertheless be comparable to losing a small library of about 150,000 books. Generally speaking, a single page from a book is valuable only because of its relationship to the pages that come before and after it. By that reasoning as well, bits of information are combined together, and their value on their own is often limited. So the loss of any one page in books (or the loss of bits on a smaller scale) could interrupt the structures of verifiable knowledge built up within the book. From this perspective 1 percent may still be too much.

Yet we must also consider that MDLs are a relatively new invention, and so they must be given time to grow and improve. One may say that they "ingest" or "consume" the collections of great libraries, but in reality they do not. In most cases a book can be scanned and then put back on the shelf of the library that owns it. The physical object still exists and can eventually be revised if the digital copy turns out to be imperfect.

One approach is to accept a certain level of imperfection; another is to expect nothing less. One hundred percent perfection is impossible, but we can still demand it. As unreasonable as this sounds, it does seem to be the best way to proceed.

STUDY 2
THE QUALITY OF GOOGLE BOOKS' METADATA

As libraries are focused on managing and organizing information so that their patrons can access it, metadata has become a useful tool. When we speak of card catalogs, call numbers, subject headings, OPACs, and cataloging, we are talking about the ways in which libraries create and use metadata. Metadata is central to the profession, to the philosophy, and to the everyday activities of a library. Without metadata, the modern library as we know it would not function. The most basic tasks—say, finding the location of *Harry Potter and the Sorcerer's Stone* on the shelves of a modestly sized library, become almost impossible without the aid of metadata.

So what is metadata? Metadata is at one level a listing of the title, author, publication date, call number, and other information of a book. Set to this use, it is a finding aid and a descriptor of the book. At a higher level metadata also indicates and subsequently describes the structure of a knowledge framework. Librarians also make assumptions about what metadata fields are more useful than others and how the books should be organized on the shelf. There are also inherent biases and cultural values built into the metadata system. As an example, one could point to the religion section in the Dewey decimal classification system, where Christianity is the bulk of the focus and religions such as Buddhism, Taoism, Islam, and Hinduism are relegated to a small section disproportionate to their global influence.

But does Dewey's classification system hold up today? Shouldn't other religions be given an equal place at the table? The metadata structures created to serve library patrons from more than a hundred years ago are showing their age and their irrelevancy to a globalized world. Increasingly, catalogers are forced to stretch and contort these classification schemes, including LCSH, MESH, and others, to meet the needs of present-day patrons.

Metadata is still very relevant today. Depending on the software an MDL uses, it may rely heavily on metadata to facilitate the searching of its collections, even when full-text search is available. An MDL may also use metadata to order results lists, to cluster together similar books, and to give patrons a brief description of the book. Metadata is also used to give the scanned image of a book a file name and possibly an accession number of some sort. People can sift through millions of books at the touch of a button, summoning up all the plays written by Shakespeare or all the books on how to grow tomatoes in the garden. Yet there is some unease about how metadata is created and used, and questions arise about its accuracy in certain systems.

James and Weiss (2012) conducted a study of Google Books' metadata in 2012. The aim was to see if Google Books had accurate metadata for items in its collection. Other scholars had described Google Books' metadata as a "train wreck."[2] Absent quantitative evidence, it was difficult to assess just how bad the train wreck was. Thus, four hundred books were randomly selected by inputting a random word from the *Oxford English Dictionary* into Google Books and then selecting a random title. The results were limited to books available in the full-view and preview modes. Next the authors compared the metadata fields for title, author, publisher, and publication date with the same information from the scanned version of the original.

The results were less than encouraging. Of sampled books, 36 percent had at least one metadata error. Of the four fields examined, there were thirty-one title errors, forty-eight author errors, eighty-three publisher errors, and forty-one publication date errors. Even factoring out the number of times Google misattributes a publisher (a rather easy thing to do given the state of the business), the other errors tally up to nearly 20 percent of all records. Obviously, these errors can lead to patrons not finding the books they are searching for. However, these metadata errors can be quite wrong and misleading: at the time of writing, in October 2013, a Google Books search for books by Edgar Allan Poe published before January 1809 yielded a surprising result. A slim volume titled *Der Rabe: Ein Gedicht von Edgar Allan Poe* is a German translation of the poem "The Raven," published in 1669 according to Google Books. Poe was born in January 1809, and the book clearly states that it was published in 1869 (see figure 10.1)

Some have contended that such errors are a result of Google Books attempting to use OCR technology and other means to automate its ingestion of books. However, Jon Orwant, a Google Books representative, reports in a blog post they

FIGURE 10.1
Der Rabe: Ein Gedicht von Edgar Allan Poe, showing erroneous
publication date at 1669, by Barclay & Co.

did not rely on these computerized methods to generate their metadata; rather, it is good old-fashioned human error.[3] Presumably Google, or its subcontractors, has a small army of people looking over the mass of scanned images it has accumulated and is manually filling in metadata fields.

In a typical library catalog one would expect to find around 10 percent of meta-data fields with errors (James and Weiss 2012). This number may seem high, but various studies reviewed by James and Weiss classified errors differently, making it difficult to find an "average error rate." For the purposes here, though, most would likely agree that the errors uncovered in Google Books were "major" and that the frequency of errors was above average. It should give us pause to think that one of the world's largest digital libraries has a metadata error rate significantly higher than most other libraries. It is easy to add this finding to the evidence that Google Books might have gone too far and too fast in its development of an MDL, or cut corners and thus produced an inferior product.

However, there is a counternarrative. Does metadata matter as much as we librarians think it does? Do we really need "data about data" when we can do full-text searching? Google would have us believe otherwise. Cataloging is an artful process. Despite its lengthy rules, it is arguably one of the most essential things a library does. This is what others might call a value-added service in business jargon. A library has many thousands, even millions, of volumes of books, but librarians have organized them and made them easy to find. Full-text searching threatens this view of the library and turns metadata—one of the central products of libraries—into an afterthought.

Whether or not one considers Google Books' metadata a train wreck, there is no denying that Google has spent more effort on getting the scans of books correct than getting the metadata correct. One shies away from ascribing a motive here, only to say that to Google Books the scans of texts seems to be the greater focus of the two. Google Books, rightly or wrongly, consciously or not, has wagered that people would benefit more from full-text searching within the books than from accurate descriptive metadata about the books. Though new and possibly revolutionary, this is an idea at odds with traditional library practices.

This is a troubling notion given the promise and hype of the semantic web, which proposes to automatically organize huge heaps of information for human consumption. Google appears to have turned away from this model of information organization. One can only speculate that this was for pragmatic and business reasons. Google's problem with generating accurate metadata is more complicated

145

than we might imagine. In some sense, it may be easier to default to the chaos of full-text searching, given the synonyms and various quirks of natural language, than it is to try to organize human thought and knowledge with metadata schema, ontologies, and controlled vocabularies.

STUDY 3
CULTURE AND MDLS

It is often taken as a given that libraries are cultural institutions, but there is not much critical examination of what that means. Which culture? How did the library acquire it? How does the library represent it? Many other such questions about how a library stores culture and provides patrons access to it could be asked.

These questions, and not necessarily their answers, are increasing in importance as MDLs and libraries develop in the twenty-first century. The book *Beyond Article 19: Libraries and Social and Cultural Rights* (Edwards and Edwards 2010) provides a good discussion of how the library's role has become better defined and more sophisticated in its relationship to cultural rights. In his chapter in the book Albarillo (2010) encourages libraries to "move away from our past history of an English-centered library practice." He is talking not just about the English language but also about the culture shared by English-speaking countries that gave rise to many of the current philosophies, theories, and practices that make modern libraries what they are.

He is also saying that we should be more aware of other cultures, and that what works in a library in London may work just as well in Wichita, but it may not function as well in Tokyo. This is the macro level of the argument. Similarly, tastes in books on a national or cultural scale are different, and people may have a different idea of what a library should be.

The micro level of the argument becomes more difficult to explain. Cultures exist in local communities and can vary widely even across just a few miles. Similarly, what one community wants from a library can be very different from what another wants. Books on surfing, for example, are likely more of interest in a public library in Honolulu than are books on snowboarding, but the opposite is probably true in Denver. Libraries reflect their local community. They do not so much store culture as they are shaped by it, often in an iterative fashion.

As mentioned in the earlier example of the Dewey decimal system and religion, libraries are not free from biases when representing cultures. But this idea of bias might not necessarily be a bad thing in every case. Libraries should be sensitive to the cultural needs of their community and develop collections accordingly.

Where the issue of cultural representation gets complicated is when considering the cultural foundation of an MDL. Who are the patrons of an MDL? One might say that it is anyone with an Internet connection, which means a sizable portion of the global population. How does an MDL fulfill its cultural obligations when many of its patrons come from such diverse cultures?

In their study on the coverage of Hawaiian and Pacific books in the collections of the University of Hawaii at Manoa, Weiss and James (2013) endeavored to raise these very issues regarding Google Books. It was apparent from the results of the study that gaps in the Google Books corpus do exist. Given those gaps, what is Google's responsibility or sense of prioritization for the digitization of such books from underrepresented groups? Further studies are surely warranted.

In the end, this discussion and approach to MDLs could point out gaps in the corpus and might help foster better coverage for the long term. However, these are considered preliminary approaches to more comprehensive studies. The authors hope readers will find more sophisticated methods for approaching this issue of diversity and the underrepresentation of important cultures.

147

STUDY 4

KEIO UNIVERSITY–GOOGLE BOOKS DIGITIZATION PARTNERSHIP

This section examines as a case study the partnership between Google Books and Keio University, in Tokyo. I conducted face-to-face interviews with three senior members of the Keio and Google digitization project at the Mita campus of Keio University, on September 20, 2013. During the interview, questions regarding the partnership were asked. Because of the proprietary nature of the Google digitization project, Keio partners had been required to sign a nondisclosure agreement. As a result, many details regarding the Google side of the project were not divulged. This study, therefore, examines only the Keio side of the partnership; as much as possible, it is meant to gather the impressions and record the experiences of the Keio University librarians and staff involved in the Google Book Search Library Project. Names, positions, and other personal information of the senior project members interviewed are not included here.

Overview

History of Keio University

Keio University, one of the most prestigious private universities in Japan, was founded in 1858 by Yukichi Fukuzawa (1835–1901), a founder of the modern Japan state (see figure 10.2).[4] In particular, he was interested in bringing Western learning to Japan in an effort to bring the country up to speed with the European and American world powers. The best way to do this, he felt, was to educate the Japanese using a model similar to the prestigious universities of Europe and America. In his article "Datsu-a-ron" (On departure from Asia), in the March 16 edition of the *Jiji Shimpo* newspaper, he writes, "It is better for us to leave the ranks of Asian nations and cast our lot with civilized nations of the West" (Fukuzawa 1996). Japan's entrance to the world stage from the 1860s through to the end of World War II follows this pattern.

The initial focus of Fukuzawa's school was on the study of Dutch, a reflection of the two-hundred-year history of trading with the Dutch in Nagasaki during the *sakoku*. This quickly changed to English because of the impact of US Admiral Perry's "gunboat diplomacy" and the treaty from 1858 that opened the country up to trade with the United States. By 1898 Keio had become a comprehensive school, with a college as well as a secondary school and an elementary school. Over the decades, major graduate and professional schools were established, including a school of medicine in 1917, a nursing school in 1918, a department of engineering in 1944, and even a law school as recently as 2004.[5]

FIGURE 10.2
Sculpture of Yukichi Fukuzawa
at Keio University.
(Photo by Andrew Weiss)

World War II brought many changes to Japan. Universities in Japan were not immune to those changes, as they were incorporated into the war effort both as research institutions and as officer recruiting grounds. For example, 83 percent of kamikaze pilots were university students, including some from Keio University (Shillony 1986). The university, like most of Tokyo, was also damaged during the firebombing by US forces (Fedman and Karacas 2012).

The university, like all of Japan, however, eventually rebuilt and recovered in the postwar decades. Keio remains one of Japan's most prestigious universities, on par with Tokyo University, Kyoto University, and Tokyo Institute of Technology.

The Keio Library—Mita Campus Media Center

The Keio Library system is one of the largest in Japan. Spread across several campuses, the library system houses nearly 4.2 million volumes. The main library on the Mita campus holds about 2.3 million volumes (www.lib.keio.ac.jp/en/). Currently, books are housed in two buildings, the newer library building and the older original library. Main stacks, special collections, digitization apparatus, servers, and administrative offices are in the new building. The old library building houses many of the stacks for older books. These are open to all students to browse. The older building also is used as a storage and setup area for the delivery of books, with both Japanese and Western-style binding, for Google Books. Keio also holds some of the rarest books of both Western civilization and Japanese culture. It is especially well known for having the only copy of an original Gutenberg bible outside of Europe or the United States.

149

Project History, Timeline, and Initial Goals

In 2006, as part of the lead-up to the 150th anniversary commemoration of Keio University's founding in 2008, the university and the library joined with Google for the Google Books Digitization project. In 2005 and 2006, Google appears to have been making efforts to recruit various institutions in Japan. However, aside from Keio, no other organizations elected to pair with Google. The official announcement of the partnership occurred on July 5, 2007, although work had begun on the project the year before.[6] The partnership became a university-wide project and was not limited merely to the library.

Since it officially started, the digitization project has contributed about one hundred thousand books, including both Western-bound books and traditional Japanese-bound books. The project does not include any of the special rare books held by Keio University. These are done in house because of their value and delicate nature.[7]

The process of digitization involved a fairly large staff. The starting point for the project was the clearance of copyright. One full-time Keio employee and four outsourced staff members are currently employed for checking Japanese copyright. Additionally, ten Keio reference librarians were assigned duties of checking for copyright clearance. If a work is cleared, then it is sent on to Google's digitization center. Although this limits the number of books available, it also completely eliminates any institutional risk.

The project employed outsourced staff for exporting the Keio Library catalog to Google Books as well. One person was hired to handle the logistics of taking books off the shelf and placing them in a staging area for shipment to an off-site digitization center. The location of this center was not divulged.

As part of the project process and workflow, senior Keio library staff wrote manuals for dealing with Edo-period books, especially *fukuro toji* (bound-pocket) books. Cleanup of metadata and errors in the Google Books corpus are constantly being monitored, and mistakes are noted and given to Google to fix. According to the Keio staff, sometimes this arrangement contributes to the slow changes applied to the corpus.

Project Results

The Keio University and Google Books Digitization Project resulted in the digitization of nearly one hundred thousand books that were cleared by the copyright checking team and sent to Google's undisclosed off-site digitization center. The types of books included all ranges of subjects and types of binding.

As a result of the copyright clearance endeavors, a large database with the information and copyright clearance status of nearly thirty thousand Japanese authors was created. The database is entirely in Japanese, however, and is likely to be of limited use to other institutions outside of Japan unless it is translated and/or transliterated. Specific project workflows were also developed and honed, some of which are described in Sato (2010), particularly project development. The complexity of the project becomes evident as high-level procedures for digitization are devised.

As far as overall satisfaction with the project results, the staff were somewhat divided on the ultimate success of the project. On the one hand, Keio staff acknowledged that they received positive feedback from users regarding the digitization of books. Patrons and users were very glad that the books could be put online. Their digitization meant that users did not have to visit Keio directly. As it is in the center of Tokyo, the university can be very difficult to access, especially for those with disabilities. Regarding this aspect of the project, users were grateful for the partnership with Google. However, in terms of working with Google itself, a few problems arose. First, as of October 2013, the Keio project members still had not received the data set and digital files created during the digitization project. Their attempts at communication are often not returned by Google. Second, errors in the records and problems with the display of the texts, including the right-to-left and up-to-down reading patterns of many traditionally published Japanese texts, often remain unresolved. It was noted by one Keio staff member that the process was ongoing and did not seem to have an end in sight. It seemed that once one problem was solved, another problem would arise.

Finally, as for goals, staff members believed that their basic goals were met in terms of actually having works digitized and placed online. However, all staff interviewed believed that the project would only truly meet its final goal once a copy of the data sets and digital files were given to them.

Finally, as for an ending point, all three of the staff members interviewed concluded that the digitization of the works requires a long-term commitment that will outlast any initial partnerships. Ending points may occur with respect to actual partnerships, but the digital collections themselves will remain unfinished. As a result of their current dissatisfaction with the Google Books digitization project, they are looking to partner with another MDL: HathiTrust.

Issues

Although staff members consider the partnership to be basically successful, there were a number of other issues raised in terms of working with Google.

Metadata and Controlled Vocabularies

Perhaps the most pressing issue was regarding the development and use of metadata in the project. To partner with Google and become interoperable with the Google Books project, Keio Library had to create records in the MARC 21 format. However, Japanese libraries generally do not use this standard. Keio was not using it, and therefore had to create new database records. Overall, staff members felt that Japanese libraries are far behind in terms of adopting Japan-wide standards and interoperability. In this sense, the project forced them to come up to speed in terms of international standards for information sharing. Though time consuming, it was a worthwhile effort in their eyes.

Additionally, the Keio staff found that the Google Books corpus contained numerous metadata errors. Problems of language and standardization of names were amplified by the sometime non-uniform transliteration practices from Japanese to English. Another issue related to metadata stems from the source materials themselves. In one problem, for example, most Japanese books were not assigned

ISBN numbers until the 1970s. This is a major element used to define the books in the Google Books corpus. As a result, specific editions contain errors.

The use of controlled vocabularies in Japanese libraries is slightly different as well. Libraries often use either the Nippon Decimal Classification (NDC) system or the National Diet Library Subject Headings (NDLSH). Only certain disciplines at Keio, such as social sciences, use the US Library of Congress Subject Headings (LCSH). Medical libraries in Japan use MESH. However, Google Books is using BISAC (Book Industry Standards and Communications) subject headings. As Nunberg has pointed out, the use of BISAC is extremely error-prone and not even used by libraries in the United States.8 Keio has also experienced exacerbated issues related to this given the crossover from Japan-centric information science fundamentals to American-centric fundamentals, which have been further altered by Google's own private interests.

Scanning Issues

Mistakes in the actual scans were also noticed. The types of problems noticed were manifold. As shown in previous studies, these issues are quite common for Google Books. First, some of the books were just not digitized very well. Fingers or hands were visible in the pages. Some pages were blurry. Some pages were upside down, and so on. Quality control was quite low, staff members felt.

Second, the digitization of Japanese traditionally bound books was not always handled in a manner appropriate for the medium. Google Books, they felt, approached every book in exactly the same way. As a result, some of the unique aspects to a traditionally bound book were lost. One example is the *gyobi* mark in the center fold of a page, also known as the fore edge, or *hanshin* (Tsuchitani and Fujishiro 2011). The running title, volume number, and folio number are usually printed in this area, too (see figure 10.3). This important information was lost during the digitization process.

Furthermore, the online display in Google Books is designed for Western books, which are read horizontally from left to right. However, many Japanese books are read from right to left and in a vertical fashion; the current reader for Google Books does not address this issue.

Also, OCR for Japanese text is very poor. An acceptable OCR program for Japanese still does not exist, according to Keio staff. As a result, most books cannot be full-text searchable in any meaningful way, regardless of their effort. It should be noted that this is not Google Books' fault. Incidentally, Keio's in-house scanned rare books do not have OCR applied to them either. Many books are also written using

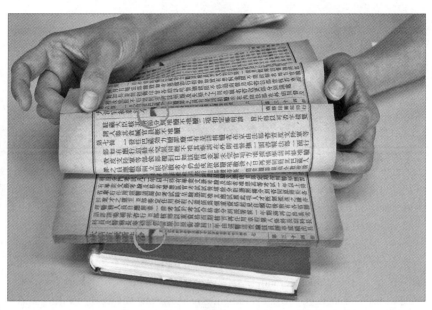

FIGURE 10.3
Image of a traditionally bound Japanese book and the *gyobi* (circled)
printed in the *hanshin,* or fore-edge, which provides information about the
publisher printed on the crease of the two sides of a single sheet of paper.
(Photo by Andrew Weiss)

a calligraphic script or font that, given the very individualized hand of the writer,
is very difficult to read and impossible for OCR programs to decipher.

Missing Files

The issue most disconcerting to Keio staff members was the fact that Google did
not return either the data sets or the digital files. While they were cognizant of the
fact that Google is operating under a for-profit business model, they felt that the
data set and scans were of great importance and should be given to them as soon
as possible. Attempts at communication with Google were also very difficult. The
project staff members felt that they were a minor partner in the overall Google
Books project and were therefore treated accordingly. The slow response times for
emails and correspondence were seen as definite negatives of the partnership. Staff
felt that it took much too long even to change the simplest things.

Also, an ending point is not in sight for them as a result of these issues. Ongoing tweaks and data support are needed. Until the digital files and data sets are

provided to staff, digital preservation remains out of their hands. They have to continue being vigilant about the display of the books, yet as they change one thing, this causes another mistake or issue to appear.

Copyright

Issues of copyright also arose in the Keio project. While US copyright law allows for works prior to 1923 to be accessible, in Japan works prior to 1943 are available for public use. This means that a larger amount of potentially public domain materials exists in Japan. However, publishers in Japan are much more protective of their interests. As a result, even works that were potentially in the public domain were not used if images or other materials within the books did not clear copyright.

In a related issue, a publisher's trademark also cannot be scanned without permission, according to Japanese law. The permissions to use the publisher's mark were often deemed too difficult to get, even though the work itself might actually have been in the public domain. As a result, quite a number of works were not added to the collection, further diminishing the number of works in the project. The need to be vigilant about the copyright clearance process and to completely ensure that a work has been vetted also slowed down the digitization as well.

Rare Books and Alternative Bindings

As a result of the rarity and the importance of many of their special collection works, the Keio Library decided to not include many eligible books in the Google Books project. First, books that were too rare to be trusted in the hands of anyone besides historical specialists with knowledge of *washi* or other traditional Japanese materials were not given to Google. Since the digitization of books via the partnership is done off-site, it was also deemed too risky to allow the books to be either shipped or taken off-site.

Second, many of the special collections also include odd-size pages (i.e., *detchoso* glued books; *tetsuyoso* sewn books; *makimono* scrolls, including *orihon* folding books), as well as three-dimensional objects, including coins, and family seals known as *kamon* (Tsuchitani and Fujishiro 2011). The Google Books project handles books bound in the Western manner, but it has trouble with the quality of scans in anything that doesn't adhere to this standard. Third, the delicacy of the materials is also a problem. The materials, especially brittle pages, might not hold up under the mass scanning procedures developed by Google.

Cultural Differences

Finally, issues of cross-cultural differences were approached during the interview. While it is true that Japanese culture can be very inward-looking and traditional, and the language can be very difficult for Westerners to master, many of the problems in the project did not seem to stem directly from these differences.

Staff viewed issues deriving from a clash of Japanese versus American or Western culture as minor. Instead, they felt that the problems of the project arose more from issues of a mass digitization or mass production culture versus one of respect and appreciation for cultural artifacts. In many ways, the project problems outlined the issues inherent to a disposable culture versus a sustainable culture.

Issues of a business culture with values not in sync with a nonprofit educational culture were also seen as contributing to some of the problems in the project. While Keio University staff expected more openness in terms of sharing of information and project results, Google's proprietary nature and its insistence upon having project partners sign nondisclosure agreements placed a damper on those expectations.

Furthermore, while the staff understood the need for some secrecy, that also contributed, they felt, to distrust among certain faculty at Keio University. These staff members saw the nondisclosure agreement as evidence that the Mita Media Center was doing something against Keio's interests.

Conclusion

The Keio-Google digitization project appears to be both partly successful and partly problematic. It is likely that the partnership between Keio and Google will go down in history as a poor example to follow for other libraries—especially those that are outside the United States. Too many problems between the American corporation and the nonprofit Japanese university existed for the satisfactory digitization of books.

Keio staff in particular strongly advise any Japanese library against partnering with Google. It's a different culture not only in terms of language and customs but also in terms of business practices and nonprofit educational endeavors. While educators are interested in sharing information, it is not always in the best interests of businesses to do the same. Full disclosure for universities is far more beneficial and far less risky than it is for a corporation like Google. This case does not bode well as a precursor to Google or other MDLs dealing with an international partnership.

Also at issue is the long-term sustainability and growth of MDLs. The inability of MDLs to bridge cultural gaps may impede both their progress and their impact. The major flaws in the Google Books project partnership with Keio shine a light on many of the cultural assumptions that the US company has made regarding its ability to digitize every single book ever created. While this sounds like youthful idealism on the part of Google's founders, at the same time it is also an impossible goal. Google appears to be approaching the project purely from the sake of a mass-digital culture, but many of the works held by Japanese institutions, and many other countries as well, have their own cultures and their own customs. The level of trust just does not seem to be there for a long-term sustainable and broad movement to really take place.

As a final thought, the concept of *teinei* in Japanese might offer a clear contrast to the Google-driven culture of mass digitization. *Teinei* is a pose of respect and care for works that have been created. It is often associated with Japanese fine arts such as the tea ceremony, papermaking, ceramics, and the like. Printed Japanese books still hold that power of craftsmanship over many individuals, including many of the faculty at Keio and as a result the distrust of the digital world among these disciplines remains high.

The current mass-digital culture does not take this attitude into account. One must wonder whether Google's IT-engineering, profit-driven approach is right for the digitization of rare and wondrous works of art. Many of these are works that require a level of calm introspection and intelligence rather than brute numbers, force, and profitability at the expense of quality. A mass digitization project approached in the Google way may be at odds with those values.

According to a press release from February 14, 2014, Keio and the HathiTrust announced the addition of eighty thousand volumes from Keio's digitized corpus into the MDL's collection.[9] Given all that we have read about the difference in approach that the HathiTrust has taken in terms of mass digitization, this promises to be a long and prosperous collaboration.

REFERENCES

Albarillo, Franz. 2010. "Cultural Rights and Language Rights in Libraries." In *Beyond Article 19: Libraries and Social and Cultural Rights*, ed. J. B. Edwards, and S. Edwards, 85–112. Duluth, MN: Litwin Books.

Edwards, J. B., and S. Edwards, eds. 2010. *Beyond Article 19: Libraries and Social and Cultural Rights*. Duluth, MN: Litwin Books.

156

Fedman, David, and Cary Karacas. 2012. "A Cartographic Fade to Black: Mapping the Destruction of Urban Japan during World War II." *Journal of Historical Geography* 38, no. 3: 306–28.

Fukuzawa, Yukichi. 1996. "Good-Bye Asia (1885)." In *Japan: A Documentary History— The Late Tokugawa Period to the Present*, ed. David John Lu, 351–53. Armonk, NY: M. E. Sharpe.

James, Ryan. 2010. "An Assessment of the Legibility of Google Books." *Journal of Access Services* 7 (4).

James, Ryan, and Andrew Weiss. 2012. "An Assessment of Google Books' Metadata." *Journal of Library Metadata* 12, no. 1: 15–22.

McEathron, S. 2010. "An Assessment of Image Quality in Geology Works from the HathiTrust Digital Library." *Geological Society of America Abstracts with Programs* 42, no. 5: 399.

Sato, Yurie. 2010. "Keio Gijuku Daigaku ni okeru Google-Library-Project no chosakuken chosa nitsuite." *Media Net*, no. 17, 51–53. www.lib.keio.ac.jp/publication/medianet/article/017/01700500.html

Shillony, Ben-Ami. 1986. "Universities and Students in Wartime Japan." *Journal of Asian Studies* 45, no. 4: 769–87.

Tsuchitani, Isamu, and Manae Fujishiro. 2011. *Descriptive Cataloging Guidelines for Pre-Meiji Japanese Books*. www.eastasianlib.org/cjm/JapaneseRareBooks-CatalogingGuidelines_Rev2011-Final%2020120205.pdf.

Weiss, Andrew, and Ryan James. 2013. "Assessing the Coverage of Hawaiian and Pacific Books in the Google Books Digitization Project." *OCLC Systems and Services* 29, no. 1: 13–21.

NOTES

1. Paul Duguid, "Inheritance and Loss? A Brief Survey of Google Books," *First Monday*, August 6, 2007, http://firstmonday.org/htbin/cgiwrap/bin/ojs/index.php/fm/article/view/1972/1847.

2. Geoffrey Nunberg, "Google Books: A Metadata Train Wreck," *Language Log* (blog), August 29, 2009, http://languagelog.ldc.upenn.edu/nll/?p=1701.

3. Geoffrey Nunberg, "Google Books: The Metadata Mess," presentation at the Google Book Settlement Conference, University of California, Berkeley, August 28, 2009, http://people.ischool.berkeley.edu/~nunberg/GBook/GoogBookMetadataSh.pdf; Geoffrey Nunberg, "Google Books: A Metadata Train Wreck," *Language Log* (blog), August 29, 2009, http://languagelog.ldc.upenn.edu/nll/?p=1701.

4. Yukichi Fukuzawa, Keio founder, www.keio.ac.jp/en/about_keio/fukuzawa.html.

5. "History," Keio University, www.keio.ac.jp/en/about_keio/history/.

6. "Keio University to Partner with Google, Inc. for Digitalization and Release of Its Library Collection to the World for Formation of Knowledge of the Digital Era," Keio University, www.keio.ac.jp/en/news/2007/070712.html.

7. S. Sugiyama, "Google Book Search Library Project at Keio University, OCLC," www.oclc.org/content/dam/research/events/2008/06-02hb.pdf.

8. Geoffrey Nunberg, "Google Books: The Metadata Mess," presentation at the Google Book Settlement Conference, University of California, Berkeley, August 28, 2009, http://people.ischool.berkeley.edu/~nunberg/GBook/GoogBookMetadataSh.pdf; Geoffrey Nunberg, "Google Books: A Metadata Train Wreck," *Language Log* (*blog*), August 29, 2009, http://languagelog.ldc.upenn.edu/nll/?p=1701.

9. "Update on January 2014 Activities," HathiTrust, www.hathitrust.org/updates_january2014.

Index

Page numbers in italics indicate a figure.